The elegant solution

JEAN FORD BRENNAN

Princeton, New Jersey   Toronto   London   Melbourne

The elegant solution

D. Van Nostrand Company, Inc.

VAN NOSTRAND REGIONAL OFFICES: *New York, Chicago, San Francisco*

D. VAN NOSTRAND COMPANY, LTD., *London*

D. VAN NOSTRAND COMPANY (Canada), LTD., *Toronto*

D. VAN NOSTRAND AUSTRALIA PTY. LTD., *Melbourne*

Library of Congress Catalog Card No. 67-27988

The preparation of this book was sponsored by the Commission on Engineering Education, Washington, D.C., and was financed in part with funds granted by the Alfred P. Sloan Foundation.

TO BILL AND BILL, JR.

foreword

REMARKABLE CHANGES have taken place in the United States during the last twenty years. These changes have enriched and improved the lives of us all. There have been many contributing forces, but among the most pervasive are new modes of travel and communication, new materials, new methods of design, synthesis, and information handling, and new sources of energy. Wherever one looks, one finds the trappings of these—the jet airliner, color television sets, picture telephones, nuclear power plants, metal and plastic skis, transistor radios, battery-powered appliances, to mention just a few. Not so evident, although equally significant, are the missiles, radars, submarines, and other weapons which are the crux of this country's defense and deterrent power. And this, really, is only the beginning; this outpouring of technological achievement continues to increase and proliferate.

All this has brought both benefits and problems to our society, but, nonetheless, the rest of the world, from the Communist world to the "underdeveloped nations," is unanimous in trying to duplicate our performance. Though some countries are making rapid progress in this endeavor, others seem unable to do so.

Hence, we are led to reflect on the real sources of our society's wealth. Clearly science and research, through the creation of new knowledge, are powerful influences. (The new knowledge thus produced has been well publicized, but still the ways of producing it are not well understood by either the public or officialdom.) Equally vital are invention, the creation of ideas which bring hitherto unthought-of arrangements to bear on specific tasks, and innovation, the process of bringing new understanding and ideas to a marketable form for society's consumption. Innovation and invention are the bedrock of good engineering—and the highway of progress. This road which engineering must follow, from the new possibility dimly seen to the actual fact in being, is often a long one, although it is now a great deal shorter than it once was. However, it still takes years to create a supersonic aircraft, an integrated-circuit computer, or an electric-drive automobile. And more than time, it takes an attitude of adventure and a willingness to change the traditional in constructive ways.

Indeed, technical progress can have its impact on society only in a receptive environment. The commitment of venture capital, private or public, must be based upon an astute assessment, not only of existing needs, but of latent ones as well. There must be rewards for the inventor, the researcher, the investor, the worker, and the administrator. Somehow, under the American socio-economic system, we have achieved both wealth and a viable, fairly stable accommodation in the apportioning of it.

This great American enterprise is a complex affair, to which no few words can do justice. However, the reader will discover many factors and interrelationships for himself in reading this book, which is an attempt to document some of the great technological achievements of our time. These accounts are as accurate as conscientious scholarship can make them, and each one represents the genesis of a development which has profoundly influenced our mode of living. Thus *The Elegant Solution* provides a backdrop for our future.

The source of inspiration for this book was the earnest desire of Dr. John R. Pierce, of the Bell Telephone Laboratories, and Dr. Fred C. Lindvall, of the California Institute of Technology, to make the facts of technological progress available to students. These facts have been little understood nor have they been publicized. Dr. Pierce and Dr. Lindvall hoped that accurate and detailed accounts of real engineering achievements would lessen the chances that political oversimplification and doctrinaire tinkering with the processes of progress would be acceptable to tomorrow's citizens—today's students.

This plan has been most ably executed by Jean Ford Brennan, whose lively style, training in research, and active concern with the technical aspects of her subject have served that subject very well. The studies to be made for this volume were selected jointly by Mrs. Brennan, Dr. Newman A. Hall, Executive Director of the Commission on Engineering Education, and myself, as a member of the Commission. In each field, a technical advisor-consultant was provided Mrs. Brennan. Because of the close association of these advisors (listed in the "Acknowledgments") with the development of the particular subjects, much valuable data was forthcoming, and authenticity was ensured. In addition, The Boeing Company, Bell Telephone Laboratories, International Business Machines Corporation, and Xerox Corporation have cooperated splendidly with Mrs. Brennan, as have many individuals associated with universities, businesses, and government. Encouragement and financial support were contributed by the Alfred P. Sloan Foundation and by the Commission on Engineering Education. To all of these people and organizations a vote of appreciation is due for their parts in bringing these cases of engineering achievement into a visible, lasting form.

EDWARD E. DAVID, JR.
Commission on Engineering Education

Bell Telephone Laboratories
Murray Hill, New Jersey
May, 1967

author's preface

IN THE WORLD OF MATHEMATICS, when the solution to a problem exhibits precision, neatness and simplicity, it is said to be "elegant." This is such a happy term that I have borrowed it for use in a different, though related, context. The pages that follow set forth a few of the curious and baffling problems that have challenged the world of engineering in recent years and attempt to show how for each of them "the elegant solution" was ultimately found. The search was usually long, frequently hard, sometimes dangerous. But for the men who had the good fortune to take part in blazing these new engineering trails, the experience was at once exciting and unforgettable.

To all those who took time from important work to relate the adventures described in this book, I should like to express my great admiration and warm thanks.

JEAN FORD BRENNAN

Ossining, New York
May, 1967

xi

contents

the
dash
80

At 4 P.M. on May 14, 1954, the great doors of the Boeing Company's Renton, Washington, hangar rolled slowly open, and there emerged into the pale spring sunlight the first jet passenger plane ever built in the United States. Propellerless, half a city block long, higher than a three-story building, with wings lowset and swept back at a startling angle, the 81-ton behemoth moved majestically into full view. Then it could be seen that from the undersides of the wings—like vestigial pontoons—there projected four cavernous, cigar-shaped pods, each of which housed a powerful jet engine.

To the spellbound onlookers, the spectacle conjured up strange and wonderful images—an enormous metallic firefly bearing four cocoons or a landlocked hybrid from the sea, half graceful dolphin, half lethal shark. To those of Boeing's management who were present, however, the plane represented one thing only: a $16-million bid to capture the huge potential market among world airlines for commercial—as well as military

1

—jet planes. On the nose of this single airplane—the Boeing 707, built behind a wall of secrecy under the code name "Dash 80"—rode not only eight years of costly developmental work by three hundred of the company's top engineers, but Boeing's reputation for excellence in plane design as well as the very financial future of the company itself.

And here was Boeing's dilemma: the airlines, unconvinced that the time was right to commit themselves to costly investment in jets for commercial service, had warily refused to place a single advance order from blueprints and models for one of the new planes. The United States Government, too, had declined to authorize production of a military version of the plane until a prototype had been built and tested. Forced either to invest its own funds in building the plane or run the risk that another manufacturer might do so, Boeing had chosen to gamble the money. Now it was up to the "Dash 80" to prove itself—the greater speed and efficiency of its jet engines, the aerodynamic advantages of its advanced airframe design, the safety and comfort of its operation. In so doing, it would prove the case for future passenger jets everywhere. As it turned out, the "Dash 80" not only resolved the Boeing dilemma, but it also opened the way for the successful launching of commercial jet aviation in the United States. To appreciate the reasons for its success, a glance at its ancestry is in order.

TWO STUDENTS—ONE IDEA

It is one of the lesser known facts of aviation history that the jet aircraft engine was invented not by experts in aerodynamics and power plant design but by two students—one in England and one in Germany. In 1928, the year after Lindbergh's 33-hour, 39-minute flight from New York to Paris, Frank Whittle, a twenty-year-old cadet at the Royal Air Force College in Cranwell, England, wrote his fourth-term science thesis on the topic, "Future Developments in Aircraft Design." In it, at a time when the top speed of British fighter planes was about 150 m.p.h., Whittle pointed out that if the achievement of great speeds up to 500 m.p.h. were to be combined with long-range operations, it would be necessary for planes of the future to fly at very great heights where the air density was less than a quarter of that at sea level. To operate at such speeds and heights, he theorized, a power plant far more adaptable than the conventional piston engine—perhaps a form of rocket propulsion or a gas turbine driving a propeller—would have to be evolved.

After turning in his paper, Whittle found himself continuing to speculate on the idea of putting a gas turbine in a plane. He knew that the fundamental principle of the gas turbine—to accomplish work by utilizing the expansive energy of heated gases —had been known from antiquity and that practical development of such an engine dated back to the nineteenth century. As a matter of fact, the gas turbine had already found a place in the aircraft industry: it was widely used to drive "superchargers," or air blowers, to increase the supply of oxygen to the cylinders of piston-plane engines, thereby facilitating flight at high altitudes. In simplest form, a gas turbine consisted of a compressor which pulled in air and increased its pressure to several times that of the atmosphere, then channelled it into a combustion chamber. In the chamber, fuel sprayed into the compressed air was ignited to create continuous combustion. The resulting large volume of high temperature gases was then directed against the blades of a turbine rotor which turned it into kinetic energy. Part of this power was used to drive a shaft connected to the air compressor and the rest was delivered to a generator, crankshaft, or other mechanism to perform work.

As Whittle considered the advantages of the simple gas turbine over the piston engine—with all its moving parts, vibration, inertia, and other complications—he was suddenly struck by the thought that instead of using the turbine's combustion products to drive a plane's propeller, they might be forced through a tail pipe into the ambient atmosphere to produce a propelling jet. Such an arrangement ought to work, he thought, for, by Newton's Third Law of Motion, action is accompanied by an equal and opposite reaction. Even after using part of the gases to drive the all-important air compressor, the velocity of the remaining gases issuing from the tail pipe would be sufficiently greater than that of air entering the compressor up front to drive the plane forward.

"Once this idea had taken shape," Whittle recalls, "it seemed rather odd that I had taken so long to arrive at a concept which had become obvious." Early in 1930, he filed for a patent on a turbo-jet engine. It called for a centrifugal type of air compressor, which produced a high pressure rise in a single stage; a combustion chamber assembly; a single-stage gas turbine something like a powerful little windmill; and an exhaust pipe ending in a jet nozzle. A shaft was to connect the rotor of the compressor to the wheel of the turbine.

Having patented his engine, Whittle persistently tried to interest the British Air Ministry in the idea of jet propulsion for military aircraft. Patiently, it was explained to the eager young man that a gas turbine in a plane was impracticable because, among other things, no materials existed which were capable of withstanding the high temperatures and high stresses involved. So little official interest was taken in Whittle's patent that it was not even placed on the secret list, but was published throughout the world in 1932—a lapse that was to cause great handwringing a decade later.

Five years passed before Whittle was able to interest private capital in backing his invention. Two more years were spent in a search for materials, special steels and aluminum alloys, suitable for use in a gas turbine. Then in 1939, as war threatened, the British Air Ministry suddenly changed its mind. After following Whittle's work with benevolent detachment for several years, it had become convinced that the turbo-jet engine was practical after all and authorized the construction of a flight engine, the W-1, and an experimental plane to put it in, the Gloster-Whittle E-28/39.

At Göttingen University in Germany, meantime, a student named Hans von Ohain* had arrived at much the same conclusions as Whittle and in the mid-1930's had invented a jet propulsion engine based on almost exactly the same principles. He arranged to have his engine patented and, with better luck than his British contemporary, succeeded in interesting the Ernst Heinkel Aircraft Company in building an engine, the He-S3B, to his design. By the late 1930's, Heinkel had also begun construction of a single-seater experimental plane, the He-178, with the jet engine mounted in the fuselage and the air intake in the nose.

THE SWEEPBACK DEVELOPMENT

Even while Whittle and von Ohain were pursuing their remarkable undergraduate careers, a third scholarly young man was at work on a development that was to make a profoundly important—though delayed—contribution to the future of jet flight. Adolph Busemann, a thirty-four-year-old member of Reichsmarshal Hermann Goering's newly created Aeronautical Research Institute at Braunschweig, had conducted a special study of high-speed airflow in relation to aircraft design and had come to some thoughtful conclusions. He postulated that, as the speed of a plane approached that of sound,** masses of air would not

* Dr. von Ohain is now Chief Scientist of the Aerospace Research Laboratories at Wright-Patterson Field.

** The ratio of a plane's airspeed to the speed of sound at a given altitude is known as its "Mach number." Thus at sea level, where the speed of sound is 763 m.p.h., a plane flying at 460 m.p.h. would have a Mach number of 0.6. At a higher altitude where the speed of sound is lower, say, 700 m.p.h., a plane flying at 630 m.p.h. would have a Mach number of 0.9.

be able to get out of the way quickly enough but would pile up before its wings, increasing drag to the point where lift would be seriously reduced.

Since a plane's "lift-to-drag" ratio is of critical importance in determining the amount of thrust (and thus fuel) required to propel its weight through the air, Busemann concluded that if long-range flight at high Mach numbers were not to be prohibitively wasteful of fuel, a substantial improvement in lift-to-drag ratio would have to be achieved. He began to experiment with wing design and, through wind tunnel tests, found that: as the thickness of the wing decreased, so did the drag; that when the width of the wing's chord (the distance from its leading to its trailing edge) was low in proportion to its span (the distance from the fuselage to tip) lift was increased; most important, that if a long, thin wing, instead of extending out at right angles to the fuselage, were swept back at an angle, its aerodynamic characteristics at very high speeds would be substantially changed. Instead of air piling up in front of the wing, creating "compressibility burble" and instability in control, it would strike the wing at an angle and flow back over it in a side-slipping effect.

Busemann checked his findings, consolidated them into a technical paper and presented them at the Volta Scientific Conference in Rome in 1935, where they stirred not a flicker of interest. To the assembled scientists, the concept of planes flying at anything like the speed of sound seemed remote to the point of irrelevance. Later, not a few of those present were to berate themselves soundly for their shortsightedness.

WAR FORCES THE ISSUE

One week to the day before the outbreak of World War II, the Germans' experimental Heinkel-178, with its 880-pound thrust von Ohain engine, made the first jet flight in history. The test is believed to have lasted only about ten minutes, but it set in motion a train of portentous events. The German military mind quickly appreciated that a jet fighter capable of flying at 300 m.p.h. or more could climb much more quickly to higher altitudes, strike, and get away faster than any piston plane possibly could. Moreover, jet planes burned kerosene instead of scarce gasoline. By the middle of the war, advanced jet engine and airframe designs had been developed and all German aircraft companies had been pressed into jet production. In 1944, Messerschmitt ME-262's with twin jet engines appeared in the skies over Germany to make slashing attacks on American Boeing Flying Fortresses bombing German cities.

Although the Germans had succeeded in putting a jet into the air nearly two years before the British first sent aloft their Gloster-Whittle E-28/39 in May, 1941, the British plane with its 855-pound-thrust W-1 engine had been much more carefully built and tested, with the result that it was far safer and more efficient than the German jet. Making up for lost time, the British Air Ministry rushed production of the Whittle engine and of Gloster Meteor fighters, and, by 1944, British jet fighters saw action over the Channel, shooting down German V-1 "buzz bombs." *

The importance of the 1941 flight tests of the E-28/39 had not been lost on United States military representatives in England. Although the United States was not then in the war, information about the plane was freely shared by the British and three months before Pearl Harbor, under an exchange agreement, a W-1 engine was flown to the United States and a set of drawings sent by sea in best cloak-and-dagger style. Shortly thereafter, General Electric Company began construction of a prototype of the engine, modified to make use of American parts, and Bell Aircraft Corporation undertook to build an experimental jet fighter. In one of the most remarkable engineering

* The first V-1 to be downed by a jet was accounted for by a Meteor pilot who, on finding that his guns were jammed, caught up to the 400 m.p.h. flying bomb and tilted it with his wing tip until it went out of control.

achievements of the war, the 1,250-pound thrust GE-IA engine was completed in less than a year and the Bell XP-59A made its successful flight tests in October, 1942. Only three years after the first jet flight, the United States had a jet plane. A year later, the Air Force ordered production of the first operational jet fighter, the Lockheed P-80 "Shooting Star," powered by a GE engine developing 4,000 pounds of thrust.

AFTERMATH

The German Army surrendered to the Allies on the morning of May 7, 1945, and that afternoon members of the U. S. Air Force Scientific Advisory Board entered the deserted laboratories of the Aeronautical Research Institute in Braunschweig—scene of Adolph Busemann's studies of a decade earlier*—where they began eagerly searching through the precise records. One of the group was George Schairer, head of the aerodynamics department of the Boeing Company. As he glanced through the files, Schairer came upon a set of drawings of a plane with its wings swept back at a startling 45-degree angle. Accompanying the drawings were charts and wind tunnel calculations—all pointing to the advantages of "sweepback" in high speed planes. As he examined the material, Schairer immediately recalled the experiments earlier in the year of R. T. Jones of the National Advisory Committee for Aeronautics on "arrowhead" wings for high-speed planes—experiments the present findings appeared to confirm. He delved further and found drawings of other planes with their jet engines placed in a peculiar position: instead of being mounted on the wings in nacelles like piston engines with propellers, the jets were slung out from under the wings on pylons—almost as an afterthought. Schairer studied the

---

* At the end of the war, Adolph Busemann came to the United States. He is now on the staff of the National Aeronautics and Space Administration at Langley Field.

material intently for a while, then dispatched an urgent message to the Boeing Company on the implications of sweepback.

Back home in Seattle, work on a high-speed bomber had been under way since September, 1943, when the Air Force had asked Boeing, designer of the indispensable B-17 and B-29, to think about plans for such a plane. After two years of work on the project, known as the XB-47, the Boeing engineers found themselves at stalemate. The Air Force demanded speeds of 400 miles an hour, but at high speed air built up in front of the wings and drag increased. As drag increased, lift was reduced and range shortened. To cut drag, the wings would have to be made extremely thin, but in that case takeoff and landing speeds would be so great that the plane would be hard to control. It was as though some essential piece of a puzzle were missing. Then Schairer's cryptic message on sweepback had arrived and, soon after, Schairer himself bringing the important material he had discovered in Braunschweig.

With great enthusiasm now, the Boeing group undertook a comprehensive new wind tunnel program to investigate ways to adapt the principles of sweepback and high aspect ratio to the wing design of the XB-47, and soon after proposed to the Air Force that the wings be set at an angle of 35 degrees to the fuselage. These alterations were expected to result in improvements in performance which would be the equivalent of a whole ton of weight saved. The Air Force was unconvinced. Sweptback wings were supposed to have very bad stall characteristics. What about that? Before this question could be answered, another arose. Where to put the engines? The plan had been to power the XB-47 with six General Electric jet engines: two pairs set in double nacelles in the wings and one pair in the tail. But the drag which this arrangement revealed in wind tunnel tests was so great that a new design was worked out to place all the engines in the body, four blasting back over the top and two from the tail, in order to obtain an uncluttered, high-speed wing. To this plan, the Air Force now objected strenuously. Fire aboard a plane was most likely to break out in the engines. Housed in the body, they would be much harder to handle in an emergency than if isolated on the wings.

Back to the drawing board went the Boeing group. Where to go from here? At this point George Schairer's researches in Germany paid off for the second time. Why not try that curious idea of hanging the jet engines in pods out from the wings? If it were done in such a way that the pods did not interfere with air flowing over the wings, lift should not be affected. And if the thickest parts of the pods were placed far enough ahead of the thickest parts of the wings, drag should be no greater than if the engines were in the body. Moreover, if all six of the engines were slung from the wings—a pair of jets from the center of each and a single jet from each tip—overall weight should be much better distributed.

No sooner was this notion entertained by the group than it moved in and captivated its hosts. As wind tunnel tests and calculations progressed through 1946 and 1947, it began to appear that not only did pod-mounting allow for exceptionally high aerodynamic performance, producing no adverse effect on Mach number, but it made for maximum engine reliability with minimal fire hazard. In addition, pod-mounting provided easy access to the engines for economical maintenance, reduced noise by isolating the engines from the fuselage, and made possible a simplified airframe design. There was even one priceless, entirely unexpected by-product discovered in the wind tunnel tests—the pods influenced the flow of air over the wings in such a way that all the bad stall characteristics of the swept wing design were eliminated. Events moved swiftly from this point. A prototype of the XB-47 was built and flown successfully in December, 1947, and nine months later the plane was ordered into production by the Air Force.

THE LOOK OF THE FUTURE

The design of the B-47 possessed that most elusive and compelling of qualities—sophisticated simplicity. Birdlike grace was in its tapering wing span, slender body, and finely-poised tail section. But hard purpose was there, too—speed, endurance, destructive power. In the confluence of its austere, intricately-calculated curved and angular surfaces might be seen the very symbol of the complex jet age itself.

Not surprisingly, the B-47 triggered off some searching appraisals both inside and outside the Boeing Company. The Air Force, which had been pressing for the design of a long-range heavy bomber powered by turbine-driven propellers now began to consider alternatives. It urged Boeing to make studies to convert the design for its B-52 turbo-prop bomber into a sweptback jet design. Meantime, reports were circulating that Pratt & Whitney Aircraft had under development a hot new turbo-jet engine, the J-57, capable of developing 10,000 pounds of thrust and said to be the most efficient jet ever built in terms of fuel consumed. By the time a group of Boeing engineers journeyed to Wright Field in the fall of 1948 to show plans for substituting jet engines for turbo-props on the B-52, they found the Air Force willing to go further in sweepback than they had anticipated. Caught by surprise, the visiting engineers repaired to a hotel room in Dayton with their drawings to consider the situation. If the Air Force wanted a big bomber with sweepback, why not give them a big B-47? Working on top of the bureau, they upped the dimensions of the medium bomber all along the line, pasted up a model plane, and stared in wonderment at the result: 165 tons of weight, 185 feet of wing span, 35 degrees of sweepback, and eight of the new 10,000-pound Pratt & Whitney

J-57's, hung in four double pods beneath the wings. To reduce the drag of the enormous wing to a minimum, it had a varying thickness ratio to improve air flow over its surface. The design of the XB-52, like that of the B-47, not only looked right, it looked preordained. The Air Force at once authorized work on a prototype to begin late in 1948.

At Boeing, meantime, the customary preoccupation with the requirements and predilections of the military had begun to give way to excited absorption with an altogether different issue. Was the time now right, at last, to consider development of a commercial jet airliner? Although the company and the entire industry had been pondering the feasibility of jet passenger planes ever since military jets first became operational, there were some formidable obstacles to the idea. Early jet engines were notoriously wasteful of fuel, and while their relative inefficiency could be justified by combat requirements, they would be highly uneconomic for commercial operations. To make efficient use of its fuel, a jet must fly at high altitudes, where air density is low and where it can reach high Mach numbers, obtaining more thrust per pound of fuel consumed. But if a plane were to fly at altitudes and speeds where its *engines* were efficient, the *plane itself* would have to be designed to perform efficiently at those same altitudes and speeds.

Although a special group of Boeing engineers under the leadership of Maynard L. Pennell, Chief of Preliminary Design, had made numerous analytical studies of the costs, safety, comfort etc. of short-, medium-, and long-range passenger jets and had made many drawing board designs of airframes around the various jet engines that were available, no optimum combination of efficient, high-thrust jet engine and efficient, high-speed airframe had yet been found. It was not until work on the B-47 was well underway in 1947 and 1948 that the key to the high-speed airframe design began to emerge. At about the same time,

Pratt & Whitney had begun development of the J-57, and almost overnight the outlook for commercial jet aviation abruptly changed.

TO BUILD OR NOT TO BUILD

While Boeing and other United States aircraft manufacturers were busily calculating the risks involved in jumping into commercial jet development, the British had already made the leap. The Labor Government, in a bid for Britain to take the world lead in the field, sponsored a program to assist airplane manufacturers in the production of experimental jet airliners. As early as 1948, Vickers had a prototype of a four-engine Viscount turbo-propeller transport in the air. In the same year, Sir Frank Whittle, who had been knighted for his wartime work on the jet aircraft engine, became technical adviser to the government-owned British Overseas Airways Corporation. The following year saw a prototype of the De Havilland Comet, a sleek, low-wing jet with 20 degrees of sweepback and four 5,000-pound thrust turbo-jet engines buried deep in its wings, flying at a cruising speed of 490 m.p.h. and at an altitude of 42,000 feet. In all, a total of 16 types of commercial jets were under development in England in 1949. At about the same time, Canada's A. V. Roe Company launched its C-102 prototype and, soon after, began trying to solicit customers among United States airlines.

Although perturbed by this situation, United States aircraft manufacturers were caught in a bind: they were individually reluctant to invest the necessary $15 to $20 million to build a commercial jet prototype, and collectively reluctant to ask for government aid to do so. At Boeing, the level of frustration was particularly high. With 12,000 wind-tunnel hours on jet tests and literally millions of engineering man-hours on jet design to its credit, Maynard Pennell's group believed itself capable of building a prototype to put all others in the shade. Indeed, plans for such a plane had already been drawn and models built, based on experience with the B-47 and the XB-52. The transport was to have wings swept back at a 35-degree angle and four Pratt & Whitney J-57 jet engines mounted on them in separate pods. It would be designed to carry 80 to 130 passengers and to fly at a cruising speed of 550 m.p.h.

No matter how fine the plan looked in model form, however, it was clearly no match for the glamorous De Havilland Comet then flashing across Europe and into Africa and Asia on well-publicized sales missions. For two full years, while pressures mounted within Boeing to invest the money in building the prototype, nothing happened. Then in 1952, the Air Force indirectly broke the log jam by calling on the aircraft industry to build faster tankers to fuel B-47 and B-52 bombers. Here now, for the first time, was a solid argument in favor of Boeing's investing money in the prototype. It would still be a gamble—the Air Force had asked for *fast* planes, not specifically jets—but, on the whole, a reasonable one. For if the prototype were built with a body adaptable for either cargo *or* passengers, it could be used for demonstration both to the military services and the airlines and—if successful—to provide performance data needed for a production-line plane.

On April 22, 1952, the Boeing Company's board of directors listened intently to the arguments, pro and con, and then voted unanimously to allocate $15 million* to the construction and initial testing of the prototype—to be known as the 707. Six months later, the Dash 80 began to take shape behind a huge fence under maximum security regulations at the Renton plant. If Boeing was to risk its neck to build the first United States passenger jet, no prying competitive eyes were going to jeopardize the investment.

* An additional million dollars was subsequently added to cover additional testing and refinements.

STRICTLY A SPECIFIC ART

How did the Boeing engineers go about translating the drawing-board plans into the aluminum and steel reality that rolled from the Renton hangar in the spring of 1954? Before he replies, George Schairer picks up a desk model of the plane and runs his finger thoughtfully along a wing. "The airplane is a working compromise of many interrelated factors. Nearly every item is arranged to accomplish more than one purpose and there are many ways to put the components together to come up with a workable airplane. The engineers' problem is to assemble them in the most advantageous manner using the tools they have to work with and the knowledge at hand. It is strictly a specific—not a general—art."

The principal tools that Maynard Pennell and his group had to work with in 1952 were the Pratt & Whitney J-57 jet engine and the thin, sweptback, high aspect-ratio wing of the B-47 and the XB-52, each a hard-won engineering triumph in its own right. The J-57 was the first production-line jet engine to climb into the 10,000-pound thrust class and to do so while consuming the least amount of fuel per pound of thrust of any jet engine produced up until that time. Both advantages were obtained by the use of *twin* axial-flow compressors* which rotated independently on shafts turned by separate gas turbines. The arrangement allowed the engine to accelerate quickly and to operate efficiently at all speeds. The greater thrust derived from the fact that the twin compressors gave a very high compression ratio (the ratio of the pressure after the air has gone through the compressor to that which it had before going through the

---

* The early centrifugal-type compressors used in the Whittle and the von Ohain engines produced a high rise of air pressure in a single stage. They were soon superseded by the many-stage axial or "straight through" compressor which pulled in a larger volume of air and compressed it much more densely, thereby increasing the combustive power of the engine. With its smaller diameter, the axial compressor made a neater package than the centrifugal type.

compressor). At such a high ratio, approximately 1⅕ pounds of thrust could be obtained from each pound of fuel consumed— a very high level of efficiency. This combination of greater engine power and greater fuel efficiency, enabling a plane to extend its range very considerably, made the J-57 an ideal power plant for long-distance flight. Moreover, the fact that the engine was in production (and in actual use on the XB-52) meant that the 707 would not have to bear the additional burden of development costs for its power plant—a most distinct advantage.

The second basic tool with which Pennell's group came armed to the task of building the 707, the sweptback wing, had been refined by Boeing over a period of five years to a high degree of sophistication for military planes. But for commercial transports, some altogether new factors had to be considered. Topping the list was the necessity to redesign the wing so that it could serve as the fuel tank for approximately 12,000 gallons of kerosene distributed in sectionalized tanks in the interspar structure of the wings. Although fuel was routinely carried in the bodies of military planes, the practice was unthinkable for commercial airlines because of the danger, to passengers, of fire resulting from crash landing or other cause. The big problem was, then, how to retain the speed of the thin wing while increasing wing thickness sufficiently to accommodate the fuel. To find the answer, various models of wing configurations were tested in more than 4,000 hours of wind-tunnel studies. When it finally came, the solution was a compromise: thicken the wing at its root next to the fuselage, then taper it off toward the tip. Sweepback would carry most of the air past the wing's edge, and even though there would be some increase in drag, there would also be some loss in weight. For, paradoxically, the thicker the wing, the thinner the aluminum plate required to build it. Savings in metal weight would help to offset the loss in speed due to increased drag. To provide maximum strength for the controls and flaps, Boeing engineers developed a honeycomb of thin aluminum sheets bonded together to form a light weight material of enormous strength.

Equally important as the design of the wing for the 707 was the matter of its placement and its relationship to the plane's landing gear. In both the B-47 and the XB-52, the wing spars passed through the top of the fuselage. The landing gear was of the bicycle type mounted on the belly—one set of wheels fore and one aft. But in the case of the 707, there were two interrelated reasons for dropping the wing spar so that it would pass through the *lower* part of the fuselage instead. First of all, the low-wing arrangement, with the cabin above, would provide much more room for passengers and baggage. Even more important, testing had shown that a low wing would make it possible to use a tricycle form of landing gear, a set of wheels attached to the rear spar of each wing and a set mounted on the body under the nose, that would retract into the body of the plane. The advantage of the tricycle gear lay in the fact that it would permit the 707 to land at all existing airports, for the enormous landing impact of the big plane on its wheels and on runways would be much more safely distributed among three sets of wheels rather than two. In addition, the tricycle-type gear weighed a full 1,000 pounds less—and could be retracted into smaller space in the body—than the double-wheel gear.

Still another advantage of the low wing was its great elasticity. Passing through the bottom of the fuselage, the wing span could be given a positive dihedral angle—an upward deflection that placed its tips farther from the ground than those of a high wing plane. The flexible structure of the wing permitted it to bend up and down during flight, enabling it to cushion the impact of turbulent air on both airframe and passengers. In sudden gusts and downdrafts, the 707's wing would be able to flex through an astonishing maximum span of 12 feet—carrying engine pods and all.

CONTROLLING THE RESULTS

The ingenious translation of the swept wing from a military to a commercial version brought with it almost an embarrassment of success. The Dash 80's wing proved to be so aerodynamically swift and clean that it tended to "float" over runways, raising serious problems of takeoff and landing control. Safety dictated that ways and means be found to increase drag for landing and augment lift for takeoff if the 707 were to be allowed to operate on runways of normal length. Calling on Boeing's forty years of experience with airfoil design, research was initiated on an advanced flap system in which leading-edge flaps on the wings would extend automatically to deflect airflow upward, increasing low-speed lift and providing excellent control. (The system worked in conjunction with the regular trailing-edge wing flap.) To increase drag for purposes of landing control, the aerodynamicists undertook development of a system of "spoilers," metal plates which could be raised hydraulically on the upper surfaces of the wings to spoil lift. When elevated at a sharp angle above the wing, the spoilers acted as air brakes, slowing the plane to permit both controlled approach to normal landings and swift descent for emergency landings. Used in conjunction with small inboard ailerons, the spoilers also provided excellent lateral control of the wings at high speeds.

Although the flap and spoiler systems were to prove highly effective in later versions of the 707, there existed an immediate major safety problem in cutting the Dash 80's speed once it hit the runway. Conventional planes used the reversible pitch propeller to do the job, with gratifying results in reduced landing accidents. Military jets used drag parachutes, a solution not at all practical for commercial jets. Theoretically, the answer appeared to lie in reversing the jet thrust, with the hot gases directed forward instead of backward from the turbine. Some work along these lines had already been initiated by the British and by some American companies, and, while the results were inconclusive, Boeing was convinced that a reliable reverse thrust mechanism would be a vital selling point.

A careful developmental program ultimately yielded the answer: metal louvers were built into the sides of the jet engines at the point in the rear where the hot gases shot back. On touchdown, the rear ends of the four engines would be closed off with clamshell doors, forcing the gases into the louvers. These would then turn the propelling jet forward and out at the sides. Used in tandem with spoilers and ordinary wheel brakes, the reverse thruster would permit the Dash 80 to operate on even very short runways. In one test, the mechanism actually stopped the prototype within 7,000 feet of touchdown *without the use of brakes—* and then moved it back a bit for good measure.

Having succeeded so admirably in imposing discipline and control on the swift wings of the 707, domesticating it for service in and out of all airports, Maynard Pennell's group now found themselves up against an awkward consequence of their achievement. People living near airports were already complaining about the whining roar of military jets taking off and landing. Clearly, this sentiment would be seriously exacerbated by commercial jet service. Some way would have to be found to quiet the engines if the plane were to prove attractive to the airlines in terms of public relations.

Research on the problem of noise control had already been undertaken by British engineers working on Rolls Royce jet engines, and a method had been developed to exhaust the gases through a cluster of nozzles instead of one, thereby dispersing their force and the turbulence they created in the ambient atmosphere. Boeing engineers now adapted this idea to the J-57 engines of the Dash 80 by devising a set of 20 large and small circular nozzles grouped in the exhaust. Fitted into the tail pipe of each of the jets, the cluster arrangement of nozzles did cut noise substantially. The accomplishment was not without its price, however, in added weight and fuel consumption and a 2 to 4 per cent reduction in total engine thrust.

CABIN IN THE SKY

By the end of World War II, high altitude flight had become commonplace, and pressurized, air-conditioned cabins were refined to permit planes to fly safely at altitudes of 30,000 feet and over. At these heights, sudden failure of a pressure system through a leak in cabin structure or other accident could usually be offset without serious consequences by a quick drop to lower altitudes. But when jets began to climb to 40,000 feet and higher, the reliability of pressurized cabins became a much more critical matter. At these altitudes, the atmospheric pressure is so low that a leak in a pressurized cabin, unless contained, could cause the higher pressure inside to explode violently outward, ripping the plane apart and hurling its passengers to their deaths.*

For the 707, the Boeing team planned a fail-safe construction that would allow the pressurized cabin to flex through innumerable low altitude–high altitude cycles without succumbing to metal fatigue. Sheets of aluminum were assembled in overlapping sections so that if one section failed, its burden would be picked up by at least two other sections. In this way, if a rip occurred, it would be contained long enough for the plane to drop to safer altitudes before further damage could occur. Since the windows of a pressurized cabin are a special danger point, the Boeing engineers designed them to be smaller than conventional types and set them in strong aluminum forgings securely fastened to the cabin frame. The panes consisted of two separate panes of acrylic plastic either one of which would with-

* The British De Havilland Comet, which went into commercial service in 1952, was withdrawn in 1954 after two disastrous high altitude explosions, attributed to rips in cabin construction caused by metal fatigue.

stand the cabin's maximum pressure of 8.6 pounds per square inch at even highest altitudes.

The cabin door, another potential trouble spot, presented a special problem. Everyone agreed that the door must open outward to prevent a pile-up of passengers in the event of an emergency. However, to keep the door from bursting open due to pressure from within, it was made larger than the door frame and fitted into it like a plug, with edges overlapping the frame. When the handle was turned, the top and bottom edges hinged inward permitting the door to open outward.

PUSHING THE PRODUCT

As the Dash 80 took form during 1953 beneath a great scaffolding in Boeing's Renton plant, the company's salesmen stepped up the tempo of their calls on the major airlines and on the military services, sounding out preferences and requirements in a jet transport plane and offering to incorporate many of these into the prototype. The potential customers were full of suggestions for everything from longer wing span, higher cruising speed, and increased cabin diameter with more seats, to assorted equipment such as cargo hoists and anti-icing systems. None, however, was yet willing to sign on the dotted line—especially after learning that a 707 would cost about $4.5 million. Then the Dash 80 made its public debut in May, 1954, and, two months later, was successfully flight-tested at an altitude of 42,000 feet and a speed of over 550 m.p.h.—faster than *fighter* jets were flying in 1945. Convinced at last, the Air Force placed orders for the first of 500 military tanker versions of the 707, and a production line for the plane, known as the KC-135, was tooled up.

In the year that followed, the 707 flew more than a hundred demonstration flights, carrying representatives of most of the major domestic and foreign airlines and serving as a test bed for all of the plane's proud innovations: the reverse thrusters, the noise suppressors, the landing gear and brakes, the electronics

Courtesy of The Boeing Company

and controls, and the myriad safety devices. Aware that commercial pilots might be curious and perhaps even apprehensive about the intricacy of the jet's controls and its great speed, Boeing invited representatives of various airlines to inspect the plane and take over its controls for test flights. Their reaction—almost to a man—was that the plane was not only simpler to handle than conventional craft, but far quieter and more maneuverable into the bargain. In October, 1955, the Dash 80 flew a round trip from Seattle to Washington, D.C., in only 8 hours at an average speed of 567 m.p.h.—a new record for any airplane over the route. Then, in the same month, Pan American Airways, eager to launch the first United States commercial jet service, broke the tense deadlock.* The company ordered 20 of the 707's and, shortly after, American Airlines followed suit, ordering 30. From that point on, the future was no longer in doubt. Boeing's long shot had paid off.

The pioneering 707 was the progenitor of a whole family of commercial and military jet transports, intercontinental as well as transcontinental and shorter-range aircraft, produced by Boeing in the decade that followed. Largely as a result of the performance of these remarkable planes, world-wide air travel increased 100 per cent between 1959 and 1965.

Today, the first United States jet airliner—the original Dash 80—still flies for Boeing, testing advanced equipment of all kinds. At the company's bustling Seattle air field it occupies a special place in the hangar—and in the esteem of all Boeing engineers who refer to it affectionately as "the Old Lady."

* Pan American took delivery of the first certificated 707 in September, 1958, and the next month inaugurated transatlantic jet service between New York and Paris.

mark I
equals
mark II

IN THE SUMMER following the end of World War II, the Manhattan District, the wartime agency which had produced the atomic bomb, invited the United States Navy, along with other branches of the armed forces and representatives of private industry, to participate in the world's first peacetime nuclear energy project, the construction of an experimental nuclear power plant. The Navy's Bureau of Ships, seeing an opportunity to evaluate nuclear power for possible use in ship propulsion, assigned a captain and four young naval officers to proceed to the huge uranium reactor plant in Oak Ridge, Tennessee, to take part in the joint effort.

To this assignment the Naval Group, as the five men came to be known, brought a variety of talents. Captain Hyman George Rickover, a 1922 graduate of the U. S. Naval Academy, had been on active duty for twenty-four years and had served during the war as chief of the electrical section of the Bureau of Ships —a post to which he devoted himself so relentlessly that his reputation as a perfectionist and stern taskmaster overshadowed his very considerable ability. The other young officers, three of whom were also Naval Academy graduates, had been chosen for their intelligence and ability from among the Bureau's top naval engineers and specialists.

The experience of the Naval Group in the decade that followed, its early recognition that nuclear energy was of critical importance to naval engineering and its long, difficult fight to design and build the world's first nuclear submarine, is the subject of this story.

"There is absolutely no other basis on which we can proceed. Mark I equals Mark II." The icy finality in the voice of the dour, white-haired Navy captain cut through an acrimonious debate that had been in progress half the night. Around a cluttered conference table, the group of young naval officers and civilians, shirt-sleeved and tie-less in the summer Washington heat, stared at the speaker in disbelief. One of them leaned forward deliberately.

"Mark I equals Mark II?" he repeated. "Are you saying that the experimental model of the power plant for the Nautilus *must be built to the same specifications as the plant that goes into the submarine itself?"*

The captain rose with an impatient gesture and reached for his bulging briefcase. "That's exactly what I'm saying. Nobody has ever built a nuclear plant for a submarine before. We're going to make all our mistakes on the Mark I model. The day the Nautilus *goes to sea on Mark II power, there's not going to be one piece of equipment, electrical circuit, pump, valve, nut or bolt on her that hasn't been tested and proved in advance. She's going to perform perfectly."*

On May 12, 1955, the world's first nuclear submarine, the *Nautilus,* put to sea from her home base in New London, Connecticut, on a 1,381-mile shakedown cruise to San Juan, Puerto Rico. She performed perfectly, breaking most of the existing speed and endurance records for submarine performance. The huge, dark green vessel, longer than a football field, made the

84-hour trip entirely under water, the longest period of time a submarine had ever remained submerged. The average underwater speed of 16 knots maintained during the cruise was the highest ever achieved by a submarine for any period longer than one hour. The passage was the fastest ever made for the distance by a submarine—even on the surface. The trip was many times longer than any ever completed by a submarine without the use of a snorkel tube to bring in fresh air from the surface.

During the next two years, the *Nautilus* proceeded to shatter the remaining submarine records. By the spring of 1957, she had logged over 60,000 miles on her original several pounds of nuclear fuel. By contrast, a conventional diesel-electric Navy sub in a like period would have logged an average of 36,000 miles and would have burned over 2,000,000 gallons of diesel oil.

With the eyes of the world watching, the *Nautilus* continued to overturn all traditional concepts of the role of the submarine in naval operations. In the spring of 1957, she cruised from New London to San Diego, surfacing only to go through the Panama Canal. The following year, she travelled from Pearl Harbor to Portland, England, passing under the polar ice cap and the geographic North Pole, thereby establishing that there was no ocean on the globe into which a nuclear submarine could not penetrate.

Today, the *Nautilus* is but one of a fleet of about sixty United States nuclear submarines, including attack and ballistic missile types. About thirty of these submarines, deployed in ocean waters around the world, are armed with Polaris missiles which can be launched from beneath the water. The 16 nuclear missiles aboard each sub have ranges of up to 2,875 miles and explosive power equivalent to many hundreds of thousands of tons of TNT apiece. Each individual submarine is thus capable of launching toward an enemy target more destructive

Official U.S. Navy Photograph

The *Nautilus'* welcome to New York after her transpolar voyage

force than was unleashed by all the bombs dropped during World War II, including those on Hiroshima and Nagasaki. In the union of the nuclear submarine and the long-range missile with nuclear warhead, the United States has found its prime deterrent to nuclear attack.

Most engineering achievements of the magnitude of the *Nautilus* are the result of an evolutionary process that begins with established theoretical concepts and gradually proceeds through a period of painstaking development. In the case of the *Nautilus,* this gestation period was ruthlessly telescoped into an interval of approximately five years, thereby creating engineering problems so varied and so complex that the search for their solution took on the aspects of a grim detective case—one with even international implications—whose final outcome was by no means certain. In the end, the strategy that "broke" the case proved to be a combination of compulsive drive, imaginative leaps, technical skill of a high order, plus the demanding dictum of the gaunt Navy captain, "Mark I equals Mark II."

THE YEAR WAS 1946 . . .

When Captain Rickover and the four other members of the Naval Group arrived at Oak Ridge on their assignment for the Bureau of Ships in the summer of 1946, none of them had more than an elementary knowledge of nuclear energy. After a few months of intensive study under the leadership of the aggressive captain, however, the group had mastered sufficient nuclear physics to investigate various proposals for naval use of nuclear energy and to make a recommendation: the most promising prospect by far was a nuclear-powered submarine. Their arguments for such a vessel were persuasive. A nuclear power plant, operating without combustion and thus requiring no oxygen, would permit a submarine to stay underwater indefinitely; highly concentrated nuclear materials would free the sub of the periodic necessity to re-fuel, thereby increasing its cruising range indefinitely; full speed could be maintained for any length of time desired. In sum, the Naval Group pointed out, a nuclear submarine would be the world's first *true* submarine, representing a giant advance over conventional types, which were tied as by an umbilical cord to fuel depots, cruised primarily on or near the surface, were capable of submerging for only short periods, and could maintain full speed underwater for only an hour or so at a time.

Having made its recommendation to both the Navy and the newly-formed Atomic Energy Commission, the Naval Group waited impatiently for authorization to proceed with the complex job of building a nuclear power plant for a submarine. Consultations with experts on nuclear power, plus some intensive homework, had convinced the group that the best results could be obtained by making use of the heat generated by uranium fission to turn water into steam which could then be used to drive turbines geared to the submarine's propeller shafts.

THE MASTER PLAN

The idea of putting a steam power plant into a submarine was not new. It had been tried before for submarine surface propulsion—and abandoned—because the temperature of the combustion process was so great that a sub was forced to cool off before it could submerge. By substituting uranium fission for the combustion of fossil material and using part of the power generated to operate air-conditioning equipment, this problem could be eliminated. Briefly, here is how the Naval Group envisioned that such a plant would work:

✔ A core consisting of a few pounds of uranium 235 would be placed in a tightly-sealed "reactor" container through which pure water would be pumped under high pressure.

✔ Uranium fission would be set off within this core by exposing it to a source of neutron particles. Since a single neutron, when absorbed into a uranium nucleus, splits the nucleus apart, releasing an average of 2½ other neutrons which promptly split other nuclei, a self-sustaining chain reaction could be produced under certain carefully controlled conditions. In the process, kinetic energy in the form of heat would be released.

✔ Control of the number of neutrons produced, and hence the rate of fission and heat generated, would be achieved by the insertion or withdrawal of control rods made of materials that absorb neutrons without fissioning themselves. The manipulation of these rods would thus slow or accelerate the chain reaction.

↙ The water circulating through the reactor would be prevented from turning to steam by keeping it under high pressure. Its temperature could thus be raised to a level far beyond its ordinary boiling point. Since the water would still be cooler than the hot reactor core, it would carry heat away from the core through a closed pipe loop to smaller pipes in a steam generator. The high temperature of the small pipes would cause other water circulating around them in the steam generator to boil, producing steam at temperatures sufficiently high to propel the submarine.

↙ The pressurized water would have other very important uses: the hydrogen atoms in the water would slow down the speed of the neutrons bombarding the uranium—a distinct advantage, since uranium nuclei are more readily split by slow than by fast neutrons. Still another function of the water would be to reflect back stray neutrons, thereby helping to block their escape from the reactor.

This ingenious power plant, known as the Submarine Thermal Reactor (STR) was espoused by Rickover with evangelical zeal. In it, he and the Naval Group saw a union of nuclear theory, applied physics, and tried-and-true engineering practice that was totally admirable.

They could not know that two long and frustrating years were to pass before official authorization to proceed with the STR would be forthcoming from Washington.

MEANTIME, IN HIGH PLACES

Opposition to the development of the nuclear submarine was made up of many factors, some practical and some emotional, and it stemmed from many sources. Within the Navy itself, there was reluctance at certain levels to any turning away from the traditional forms of ship propulsion, especially for the purpose of furthering a submarine program and with it the career of an individual officer. In the ranks of the Atomic Energy Commission, some members were opposed as a matter of principle to the allocation of fissionable materials to another military weapon. Private industry, for its part, held back from committing substantial funds to the largely-unknown area of nuclear power production. But, above all, people generally were tired of war. Vast apathy greeted schemes for the development of new weapons—defensive or otherwise.

It took the passage of time, renewed interest in nuclear energy as a power source, and Captain Rickover's skill at political infighting, fund-wangling, and manipulating people—while simultaneously enlisting their fierce support—to produce a breakthrough. By the beginning of 1949, the obstacles had begun to disappear. The A.E.C. had authorized development of the STR at its Argonne National Laboratory. Westinghouse Electric Corporation had contracted to work with Argonne to build the reactor and the heat transfer system. Rickover had succeeded in persuading the Bureau of Ships to create a Nuclear Power Division and the A.E.C. to set up a Naval Reactors Branch and had managed further to get himself appointed head of both. He moved quickly to convert this toehold into a position from which he could then control all business of importance relating to the nuclear submarine.

Having survived the long, bitter political and economic wars, the Naval Group, reinforced with additional personnel, turned with relief to the job of getting the STR off paper and into action. A breakdown of the costs ultimately involved in work on the STR showed that of the total, metallurgical engineers accounted for 36.8 per cent, mechanical engineers 28.1 per cent, electric and electronic engineers 11.3 per cent, physicists 11.2 per cent, chemists and chemical engineers 6.9 per cent and other specialists 5.7 per cent. It soon became clear, however, that the real battle for the nuclear submarine, the engineering engagement, had not even been joined.

THE MYSTERIOUS METALS

"At the beginning of the work on STR," recalls one of the Naval Group, "we thought we knew what the problems were and that our job would be to find the answers. We quickly discovered that we didn't even know the problems."

It had been generally agreed that the key to reducing a nuclear power plant to a size small enough to fit into a submarine hull lay in the use of a concentrated core of enriched uranium 235 in the form of a gridwork of fuel elements through which the water coolant could circulate. The high rate of heat generated per unit volume of the fuel material was expected to result in high heat transfer from the surface of the fuel elements to the coolant and thence to the steam system.

In practice, there were serious difficulties in this concept. The exposure of uranium to water would corrode it rapidly, reducing the heat transfer capability of the fuel elements as well as the life expectancy of the whole fuel core. It would also produce fission products, contaminating the water coolant with radioactive material. Furthermore, as a material to be fabricated into fuel elements, uranium was very unsatisfactory.

The solution appeared to lie in jacketing the uranium with another structural metal, one which would not absorb neutrons (and thus slow the fission process), which would be highly resistant to corrosion, able to withstand extreme heat, and at the same time easy to fabricate. Well and good. But was there such a material?

Methodically, the metallurgists checked down the list of all known materials. Beryllium, scoring high in most respects, was the devil to fabricate. Aluminum, generally acceptable, corroded easily and became soft at high temperatures. One metal, a laboratory curiosity known as zirconium, seemed promising, but published figures disagreed as to its neutron absorption. Then a physicist at Oak Ridge decided to conduct further tests on zirconium and discovered to his gratification that the presence of another metal, know as hafnium, with high neutron absorption properties, had masked zirconium's real score. Purified of hafnium, with which it normally occurs in nature, refined zirconium proved to have an extremely low neutron-absorption rate.

Unfortunately, processed zirconium had such limited commercial use in the United States—small quantities in various forms were going into such things as fireworks and poison ivy ointment—that its 1948 production was only 86 pounds, and its price a high $200 per pound. Rickover promptly went into action. He had a zirconium refinery built and efficient processes worked out for separating zirconium from hafnium and for producing high-purity metal by the ton. To cut zirconium's cost and improve its fabricating properties, a combination of zirconium and uranium for use as a core material was developed.

All of this effort was still only half of the job. Zirconium had never been forged, rolled, extruded, welded, or fabricated into fuel elements or other structural shapes, and all of these metal-working techniques had to be developed from scratch. Rickover now went to work on Westinghouse Electric Corporation to give top priority to a zirconium fabrication program. In short order, the necessary machinery was installed, and zirconium fuel elements and other parts were fabricated to the desired specifications. (When asked later how the company had managed to acquire the machinery so fast, a harried Westinghouse executive answered simply, "Rickover made us get it.")

As the work on zirconium moved into high gear, another metallurgical problem—of exactly the opposite kind—presented itself. For some time, a search had been under way for a metal with an exceptionally *high* neutron-absorption rate which could be adapted for use as control rods to *slow down* the fission process in the reactor. Recalling that hafnium's neutron absorption properties had caused a false evaluation of zirconium in this regard, and that the metal had been stockpiled ever since the process for separating it from zirconium had been in production, the physicists and metallurgists applied themselves diligently to learning more about the obscure metal.

Discovered in 1922, hafnium had even fewer commercial uses than its cousin zirconium and its properties were largely unknown. For use inside a reactor, however, it turned out to have some absolutely unique advantages. Not only was it extremely resistant to heat and corrosion, but its high absorption of neutrons had the effect of producing isotopes of hafnium with equally large neutron appetites, thereby insuring long life for control rods made of the metal. In addition, it could be used in its natural, unalloyed state without jacketing. However, as in the case of zirconium, no one had ever tried to fabricate hafnium before. Techniques of melting, forging, rolling, and welding it into components had to be worked out—a task which also was assigned primarily to Westinghouse.

THE KEY PROBLEM

While the physicists and metallurgists were busy with the mysteries of zirconium and hafnium, other engineers in the Naval Group in mid-1949 were wrestling with the design of the reactor vessel, which was to contain the uranium core, the pressurized water coolant, and the control rods. An early estimate of the size of the vessel, developed at Oak Ridge and in the Argonne Laboratory, had proved too small to accommodate control mechanisms and other parts requiring space on top of the reactor core. Moreover, under certain conditions a fission product known as xenon was produced which absorbed neutrons at such a tremendous rate that reactivity was seriously reduced. However, when the size of the reactor vessel was doubled and the volume of coolant enlarged, the xenon problem proved to be controllable.

In this new impregnable container, the water coolant could be subjected to very high pressure to keep it from boiling at temperatures of hundreds of degrees Fahrenheit. An absolutely leak-proof top for the vessel was provided by means of a thin seal weld membrane applied at the closure; the whole top section was then bolted to the bottom.

Implicit in this design were two very important, and by no means routine, assumptions: first, that the pumps and valves needed to circulate the water coolant through the reactor and the closed pipe loop leading to the steam generator could be made as leak-proof as the vessel itself; second, that all parts coming into contact with the radioactive coolant—valves, pipes, etc.—would be able to withstand its high temperature and corrosive effects. Since no other lubricant except the hot water itself could be provided for the moving parts inside the closed pressurized system, it was of the greatest importance that these parts should be able to perform in such an extreme environment without failure.

On the trail of leaks and corrosion

In the search for a leak-proof pump, the engineers of the Naval Group pursued so many false scents and wound up in so many blind alleys, that they sometimes despaired of finding a solution at all. Dozens of pumps, with a variety of supposedly perfect seals, were put to the test. One by one, they failed. It seemed that the differential between the high pressure of the water coolant circulating through the pumps and the much lower pressure outside the pump housings would eventually cause any type of seal to fail. After much dogged effort, came the solution: put the entire pump, housing and all, into the pressure loop along with the reactor vessel, the coolant, and the steam generator, thus eliminating the sealing problem and, therefore, the leaks.

So far, so good. But how to operate pumps inside permanently enclosed pipe? Months later came the answer: put canned rotary pumps into the pipe loop and then transmit power *electromagnetically* from outside the loop to the pump rotors inside of it. This admirable solution also suggested one for the equally difficult problem of how to control valves inside the reactor regulating the flow of water through it. A power source *outside* the pressure system was also used to control the operation of valves *inside* it by transmitting electromagnetic power through to the plungers which operated the valve gates.

Meantime, the difficulties posed by the corrosion problem were creating dilemmas among the chemical engineers for which there was, literally, no precedent. Although special alloys with great resistance to hot water corrosion had been carefully selected and tested for use in fuel elements, pump parts, valves, etc., corrosion products continued to form on the uranium-zirconium core and to be carried to all parts of the pressure loop, increasing the radioactivity of the whole system. The seriousness of this situation was apparent to everybody. The whole point of putting a nuclear power plant into a submarine was to insure a virtually inexhaustible supply of dependable power to permit the ship to cruise indefinitely. If it developed that the nuclear fuel core could not operate for more than a limited time without having to be replaced on account of corrosion, the entire concept of the nuclear submarine would be negated.

Since the answer could not be found in any of the standard chemistry books, the engineers plunged into a study of corrosion chemistry so detailed that their findings eventually became a treatise on the subject. It appeared, in the end, that the only possible answer lay in continuous purification of the coolant water and that the way to do this was by means of chemical ion exchange.

THE ELEMENT OF DANGER

Even before the design of the various parts of the reactor compartment—the reactor vessel with its uranium core, the water coolant loop, the steam generator, the pumps, and the water purifier—had begun to take shape, the question of how to shield the submarine's crew from radioactivity in the form of gamma rays and neutrons emanating from the compartment had become pressing. The increase in the size of the reactor vessel over earlier estimates had already added considerably to the height and weight of the whole Submarine Thermal Reactor plant. This, in turn, had caused an increase in the projected diameter and, hence, the length of the submarine. Since a sub must weigh the same as water, 1 ton per 35 cubic feet, in order to maintain equilibrium when submerged, any great added weight in the form of heavy shielding around the reactor would affect its buoyancy. And, since the shielding would have to extend up high in the hull in order to enclose the reactor, creating problems of weight distribution, the submarine's stability on the surface would be lessened.

During the wartime development of the atomic bomb, land-based nuclear fission operations had been encased in thick concrete housing. Obviously an entirely different approach to shielding would have to be taken for a submarine. Among the engineers who went to work on the assignment, two philosophies soon developed. One group favored packing every piece of equipment that came in contact with radioactive elements in any degree into a single, compact block, making use of parts with the least radioactive exposure to shield those with the most, and covering the whole with a blanket of lead. In this way, a minimum of shielding would cover a maximum of equipment. Although heavy, lead was known to be effective in containing radiation because of its high density.

This view was opposed by other engineers, including Rickover, who saw that if any part inside the "package" gave trouble, it would necessitate pulling out much of the rest to get to it. This group proposed instead to place the components in the reactor compartment in an order accessible for easy maintenance behind a shield made of lead and lightweight polyethylene plastic. The nonradioactive steam line leading from the steam generator would pass through a bulkhead into a separate unshielded engine room compartment containing the condenser, turbine, gears, etc.

The idea of using polyethylene was stimulated by the plastic's high content of hydrogen atoms per unit volume. Since hydrogen atoms in water were known to have the ability to slow down and absorb neutrons, and since polyethylene contains more hydrogen atoms than water, the material seemed to possess most of the qualities needed for neutron shielding. In addition, lead and polyethylene made a more effective gamma ray shield than lead alone. Together, the two materials were expected to provide safe shielding for the crew while reducing the weight involved very considerably. On the basis of these considerations, the decision was made to proceed with the lead and polyethylene shielding—a very important move, as it later turned out.

Secret of the landlocked submarine

By early 1950, the engineers of the Naval Group, Westinghouse, and the A.E.C.'s Argonne Laboratory had progressed far enough with preliminary work on the STR to consider the next step. Captain Rickover proposed that this should be the construction on land of a full-scale prototype of the submarine plant, to be known as STR-Mark I, which would be put into operation for design and testing purposes. It was to be followed by construction of STR-Mark II, the actual seagoing plant, which would embody, step-by-step, the design changes and improvements resulting from experience with Mark I.

Although prototype construction of this sort was commonplace procedure in the aircraft and other industries, it was far from usual in the U. S. Navy. A ship with new equipment aboard usually went to sea, tested it for a period of time, and subsequently reported the results. It was not surprising, therefore, that caustic comments were heard in certain naval quarters when it became known that Captain Rickover was planning to build two complete, costly submarine propulsion plants for the controversial *Nautilus*—one for testing and one for going to sea.

Fortunately, controversy seldom daunted the captain, for opposition of a more serious kind appeared from various other sources. Engineers at Argonne Laboratory had originally planned to build the land-based Mark I in an "exploded" fashion, with all parts spread out over an area providing easy access for repairs, modifications, testing, and replacement. Later on, after all the "bugs" were out, they figured, the plant could be rebuilt to fit into a submarine hull. Rickover immediately vetoed this plan. It would take much too long if the *Nautilus* was to be at sea in five years. Mark I would have to be constructed from the start inside a submarine hull, complete with a surrounding tank of water, and on the assumption that it was a true seagoing power plant. No engineering simplifications were to be allowed.

Protesting that such a scheme was unrealistic, fantastic, and, indeed, impossible at such an early stage, a number of Argonne and Westinghouse engineers argued for the original plan. Then one hot night around a conference table in Washington, Rickover had the last word. "Mark I," he said inexorably, "equals Mark II."

One argument was ended, but another promptly flared. Where was the land-based Mark I to be built? The A.E.C. suggested that, for reasons of safety in case of an accident involving radioactive materials, the plant should be built at its reactor testing station near Arco in the Idaho desert. Most of the companies involved in making equipment and parts for Mark I opposed this idea vehemently, foreseeing the problems of transportation, communication, and general inconvenience involved. They, too, were overruled.

Gloomily contemplating the plan to which they were all committed—to build parts for a land-locked submarine in the middle of a desert 2,000 miles away—Westinghouse and the other companies took what comfort they could from the fact that Electric Boat Company of Groton, Connecticut, an experienced submarine designer and builder, had been chosen as subcontractor to build the submarine and share responsibility for adapting all equipment to the special requirements of submarine service.

By the summer of 1950, President Harry S. Truman had formally authorized the construction of the U.S.S. *Nautilus* and a tall, hangar-like concrete structure emerged starkly from the desert of the Snake River plain west of Idaho Falls. Inside the carefully-guarded building, immersed in a sea tank containing 385,000 gallons of water, was a section of the hull of a full-scale submarine. Down in the hull, Mark I was taking shape. The whole thing seemed much more like a huge toy in an enormous bathtub than the secret and deadly serious proving ground for engineering decisions that were to affect the future history of the United States Navy.

ELEVENTH-HOUR SETBACK

It had been determined some time earlier that for several interrelated reasons a certain specified limit would be placed on the projected diameter of the *Nautilus*. As work on the reactor vessel for Mark I had proceeded, its size had been increased several times in order to overcome operational problems of one kind or another. Each time, it had been necessary to enlarge the projected diameter of the hull to accommodate the larger reactor. In a submarine, an increase in the diameter of the hull must be accompanied by an increase in the thickness of the steel hull plates if the vessel is to withstand the tremendous pressure exerted on its surface by the sea. At a depth of 400 feet, for instance, each square inch of the *Nautilus* would be under nearly 180 pounds of pressure. On the whole submarine, the total weight would amount to hundreds of thousands of tons. In order to keep the *Nautilus* down to a practical size, and avoid the fabrication problems involved in increasing the thickness of the hull plates, the size of the reactor vessel could not be allowed to increase any further.

It was with considerable dismay, then, that the Mark I engineers discovered that when they started testing the control mechanisms meant for installation in the reactor vessel in the hull of the landlocked submarine, they ran into space problems in attempting to gain maximum control over fission. Although it had looked great on paper, the assembly was unreliable mechanically and complex in operation. Because of the limited amount of space on top of the reactor, the control rods were difficult to manipulate. Moreover, since no provision had been made for replacing parts in the control system, the failure of one part in a set would fail the set and, since the sets were interdependent, the failure of one set would fail the whole reactor.

It was inevitable that the practical Rickover would refuse to tolerate so complicated a set-up. Over the vigorous protests of the engineers who had labored long to develop it, he threw out the design and ordered a new system to be created, tested, and installed as quickly as possible. The result was a brilliant eleventh-hour intensive crash program which produced a system with interchangeable parts, and rods designed to save space—a solution which the engineers of the original design were the first to admit was an indispensable contribution to the development of Mark I.

Although the basic control system for the reactor was moving toward satisfactory solution, the engineers, ever conscious that they were working with a form of power never before harnessed, grew uneasy that, in actual operation, unforeseen and highly dangerous conditions might develop in the reactor. Suppose, they asked, that "hot spots" due to variables in the fuel elements built up in the core, creating heat beyond the capacity of the coolant to carry it over to the steam system. Would the reactor overheat and blow up? Suppose the pressure system fell off and the water coolant started to boil. Would it destroy the core? What if radioactivity grew more rapidly than had been anticipated—would the shielding be sufficient to contain it?

In order to have constant information on conditions within the reactor, making it possible to close it down or "scram" it in an emergency, the engineers went to work to devise instruments to indicate temperature, pressure, and flow of the coolant, radioactivity in the coolant loop, and other vital information and to transmit these data to control and power equipment outside the reactor. A system of duplicate safety circuits was devised to anticipate any dangerous instability of the reactor and to close it down automatically within a fraction of a second.

AFOUL OF EFFICIENCY

While the herculean task of designing and installing the Mark I, of containing its fission products, of shielding against its radiation hazards, and of creating for it a fail-safe control system was taxing the skills and the nervous systems of the Naval Group, work was proceeding on what was expected to be—by contrast —the more or less routine assignment of installing in the hull the steam generating system and its auxiliary machinery. What no one, including Rickover himself, could have foreseen was that in actual operation, there were to be more headaches in connection with the steam system than with the reactor itself. In a nutshell, the problems arose from the difference between operating a steam plant at sea level and operating it at more than 400 feet down in the ocean within the narrow confines of a submarine hull.

Initially, one of the prime advantages that the Naval Group had seen in the concept of hooking up a nuclear reactor with a steam plant was that it opened the door to low-temperature power production—a most desirable condition for prolonged underwater operations. Where conventional steam plants, burning fossil fuel, operate efficiently at steam temperatures of about 1100° F., it was possible to keep the steam temperature in a nuclear propulsion plant below this temperature and still generate adequate power. The employment of low-temperature steam, in turn, made possible the elimination of heavy superheaters and other conventional steam plant equipment.

Several different thermodynamic cycles for Mark I were considered and discarded by the Naval Group before they settled on one which appeared to produce best results. Although actual figures are classified, it worked something like this: by controlling the fission process in the reactor, the heat at the fuel elements would be established. The primary water coolant, under high pressure to keep it from boiling, would circulate through the reactor, pick up heat from the core, and enter the forward end of the steam generator. Secondary water in the steam generator, under much less pressure and at a lower temperature, would pick up heat from the primary coolant, boil and form steam to drive the steam turbine and generate electricity.

Well pleased with this plan, the engineers of the Naval Group took it to the Bureau of Ships for review. Their reception was icy. Sputtered one indignant senior officer: "Why, you've set back the steam turbine fifty years!" In their drive to create a steam plant suited to a nuclear submarine, the engineers had fallen afoul of a prime tenet of Navy dogma, i.e., the higher the heat and pressure generated by a naval propulsion steam plant, the greater the efficiency in terms of cruising range and fuel consumed. This had been the rule ever since the introduction of the coal-fired boiler at the turn of the century. Why should it be thrown overboard, like so much ballast, now?

Eagerly the Naval Group pointed out that, in a nuclear submarine, the reactor core, for all practical purposes, provides an unlimited supply of fuel, making possible an almost indefinite cruising range, and that, therefore, the reasons for aiming at top efficiency through high-temperature operations were no longer valid. Unconvinced, the conservatives at the Bureau felt that, once more, Captain Rickover and his group had trifled with proven marine engineering principles. Certain that he was right, Rickover overruled their objections.

PROBING FOR WEAKNESSES

As Mark I moved into its final phase of development back at Arco, Idaho, engineers of Electric Boat Co. and Westinghouse were at work installing the various components of the steam generating equipment, the engine room propulsion machinery, and the maze of pipes connecting with them. Hundreds of feet of piping were necessary to carry feedwater to the steam generator, steam to the main turbine, exhausted steam to the condenser, condenser discharge back to the feedwater tank, and so forth. When the *Nautilus* went to sea, a portion of its piping system would carry sea water at enormous pressure directly from the ocean to cool such hot spots as the steam condenser and other equipment. In this salt water system alone, as it bent and curved through the hull, were thousands of pipe joints, some of which were welded and some silver-brazed. Since all piping and joints as well as propeller shaft seals and other parts subject to sea pressure within the hull were potential hazards, pains were taken to test them under conditions simulating pressures at the greatest depths to which the *Nautilus* would dive.*

* In the first full-power test of Mark I, failure of a pipe in the steam condenser caused a serious loss of steam pressure. It is generally believed that a pipe failure may have contributed to the loss of the U. S. atomic submarine *Thresher* in April, 1963.

Since the main components of the steam plant for Mark I were conventional pieces of equipment made in quantity for years by United States manufacturers, special adaptation of such equipment was at first deemed unnecessary. It was soon discovered, however, that the main steam condenser had to be extensively redesigned for operation under sea pressure. Other standard parts, when tested under seagoing conditions, provided further surprises. The steam generator, pumps, gears, valves, and cooling system components all proved to require revision to withstand the strains placed on them by the continuous, high-speed operations made possible by nuclear propulsion. It was also discovered that the heat generated by the ship's propulsion machinery would require more air-conditioning equipment to handle it than had originally been planned. Rickover, over strenuous objections that additional equipment would add seriously to the weight of the ship, ordered several more units.

All through 1951 and 1952, Rickover pursued his goal of engineering excellence. As the time drew near to test Mark I in action at Arco, as Mark II's design proceeded at Westinghouse, and as the *Nautilus* herself began to take shape at Electric Boat, Rickover insisted on proving out everything on Mark I that could be proved in advance. Even Rickover's staunchest supporters had to agree that, in the words of one of them, "The Navy needs one Rickover, but it could never stand two." The strain which his intensive approach placed on the engineering staff during this period often flared into open controversy. Why, they asked, must *all* the problems—big and little—from getting nuclear power for the first time down to a leak in the smallest pipe joint, have to be solved simultaneously? Was this "Mark I equals Mark II" perfectionism really necessary or was it a form of compulsion?

Far from lessening his demands, Rickover responded by increasing them. "Mark II does *not* equal Mark I," he now said. "Mark II must be better in every practicable way." No longer satisfied with the testing of individual parts, then of the parts combined into systems, then of the systems together, he determined to test the total submarine design under combat conditions. He ordered several small-scale models of the *Nautilus* built and equipped with miniature pieces of machinery, arranged as they were to be aboard the submarine itself. He then had them submerged and blasted with small depth charges. After studying the results of the tests, he immediately ordered the redesign of some of the parts and the rearrangement of others, including the shielding around the reactor.

But Rickover's greatest opportunity to test Mark I equipment came when the Navy decided to sink World War II submarine *Ulua* in Chesapeake Bay and blast it with full-scale depth charges to test the vulnerability of modern submarines under battle conditions. He wangled a compartment on the submarine for use by the Naval Reactors Branch and filled it with pieces of especially vital Mark I equipment. After the demolition, when the contents of the battered *Ulua* were analyzed, it was found that the amount of shock involved was substantially greater than had been anticipated. Rickover called on the carpet several manufacturers whose "junk" (as he called it) had performed poorly and demanded that specifications for the various parts be revised upwards to insure reliability under battle stress. He gave them a time schedule which, on examination, proved to require work around the clock and over weekends as well.

REVOLUTIONARY ENOUGH

During the summer of 1952, following its keel-laying ceremony in June, the *Nautilus* began to grow on the ways of Electric Boat's Groton shipyards. The design of the submarine itself was not particularly unusual. Engineers at the Navy's Bureau of Ships, although tempted to sponsor a revolutionary design for the first nuclear submarine, decided that the *Nautilus* was already quite revolutionary enough. The simple design they came up with featured a rounded bow to improve underwater performance, and a smooth pod above the hull to enclose the usual protruding radio and radar masts and other deck-mounted equipment. Most of the hull would be single, made of exceptionally thick steel. The overall double hull of conventional submarines, designed to carry fuel oil between, would be eliminated, except in two restricted areas, and the space saved would serve to accommodate the reactor.

Thus streamlined, the *Nautilus* would be able to move faster underwater than on the surface, since its energy would be used entirely to overcome the resistance of the water instead of being partially dissipated in making great waves on the surface. Slightly longer and much heavier than conventional submarines, she would be a combatant submarine with six, 21-inch torpedo tubes in her bow. Over half of the inside space would be occupied by the reactor compartment and the engine room, including two small diesel-electric engines for emergency use.

One vital new feature was provided for the *Nautilus* by the engineers of the Bureau of Ships. This was a complete air purification system—a necessity for a submarine designed to operate primarily underwater. Although equipped with an ordinary snorkel tube to draw in air from the surface, the *Nautilus* would be able to operate completely independently of it. In the two-step purification process, a device known as a CO_2 "scrubber" operates continually to keep the level of carbon dioxide in the air within safe limits; it is supplemented by oxygen stored in a bank of tanks and fed into the submarine's atmosphere as required.

COUNTDOWN BLUES

By the end of March, 1953, Mark I was pronounced ready to start producing nuclear power. The time had come to throw the switch. Hundreds of engineers in many fields of specialization had done all that could be done to guarantee—or make it reasonably certain, or probable, or even a good bet—that no vital detail had been overlooked. And now a certain uneasiness and tension began to build up among the engineers at Arco. A member of the Naval Group commented, "At one time or another, there probably wasn't one of us who didn't have serious doubts about whether the reactor would turn out to be a workable proposition." Even Rickover at one point remarked to a fellow engineer, "If the *Nautilus* makes two knots on nuclear propulsion she will be a success."

One especially sharp sinking spell occurred when a sample of a Mark I fuel element which had been tested by exposure to irradiation for several months in the Canadian reactor at Chalk River, Ontario, was found on examination to be literally covered with "crud," or corrosion products. The test results raised serious doubts about whether the Mark I core might transfer heat for only a short time, then clog up, overheat, and fail the reactor.

Thus it was that on March 30, the day chosen to put Mark I on stream, Rickover and the other engineers hovered anxiously over the reactor controls, checking and rechecking instrument readings. Gingerly, the hafnium rods were withdrawn and various other mechanisms adjusted. Cautiously, at last, the fission process was permitted to begin. There was no explosion. No smoke curled ominously from the reactor compartment. No dial needles wagged insanely. By eleven o'clock that night, a self-sustained nuclear chain reaction was safely under way.

Although the start-up of the Mark I reactor marked the world's first production of significant quantities of useful power from nuclear energy, and was duly reported to the press by the Atomic Energy Commission in Washington, it attracted very little attention. Rickover and his group were not sorry. There was a very big difference, they knew, between starting the reactor and hooking it up to the steam power plant. Many anxious weeks, filled with many imponderables, still lay ahead.

One major imponderable was the touchy nature of the duplicate safety circuits designed to shut down the reactor in an emergency. So sensitive were these controls that Mark I could be caused to "scram" by even minor electrical or other disturbances. Obviously, a submarine's propulsion system could not be dependent on so delicately balanced a mechanism.

By May 31, after the crews at Arco had repeatedly practiced opening the main turbine throttle valve to admit steam from the generator and had rehearsed all steps to take in an emergency, the big moment arrived. The throttle valve was opened in earnest, the steam poured into the turbine, and the propeller shaft, connected to a dynamo, began to turn. After a two-hour run, during which several thousand horsepower was developed, the operation was pronounced a success.

Although Rickover and the Naval Group were profoundly relieved by the successful test run of Mark I, they were too experienced to throw their hats in the air. One big question, the most important of all, still remained unanswered. Could Mark I stand up under full power, sustained operation? During the next month, Rickover called for a gradual, step-by-step build-up of power, keeping all parts of Mark I under close observation for any sign of instability. In this period, several heartening facts emerged. Mark I was a calm, stable plant. As a result, it was possible to reduce to a minimum the number of safety circuits causing the reactor to "scram." Radiation levels were less than those anticipated and well within the safety limits of the reactor shielding.

DRAMA IN THE DESERT

On June 25, 1953, Mark I reached its full design power and the operating crews began a 48-hour test run at maximum rating. At the end of 24 hours, satisfied that sufficient data had been obtained to prove Mark I's dependability under full power operation, the engineers gave the word to shut down the plant.* Rickover, on learning of the order, promptly overruled it. He had already decided that even at the end of the complete 48-hour test, if all went well, the plant should be kept wide open until it had simulated a full-power run completely across the Atlantic Ocean. Such a dramatic test, he felt, would put to rest any lingering doubts about the advantages of nuclear power for naval propulsion.

During the next few days, a tense and curious drama, half cliff-hanger and half morality play, was acted out in the control room of the Mark I in the Idaho desert. Rickover, over the strenuous objections of other engineers, the senior naval officer at the site, the Westinghouse manager responsible for the operation of the $30 million prototype, and members of the Bureau of Ships in Washington, gambled that Mark I could run the equivalent of 2,500 miles at top power without breaking to pieces. Calling for charts of the North Atlantic, he ordered that a great circle route from Nova Scotia to Ireland be plotted. As the imaginary cruise proceeded, the position of the ship was to be calculated after each four-hour watch and marked on the charts.

As suspense grew with each succeeding watch, the cruelly sophisticated imaginations of the engineers began to produce nightmares of "crud" build-up, heat transfer failure, pump breakdown, and other assorted disasters. The crews, tip-toeing about, listened nervously for unusual noises from the machinery. At the 60-hour point, the instruments providing data on conditions in the reactor suddenly began to perform erratically, and it was no longer possible to know what was going on inside the reactor compartment. A fretful whine from one of the pumps in the coolant loop agitated everyone. At the 65-hour point, a

---

* The navy required only 4 hours at full power for acceptance of surface ship propulsion units.

pipe in the main steam condenser failed, causing a rapid loss of steam pressure. Now the demands grew urgent that the test be halted instantly. Grave warnings came from Washington. To them all, Rickover replied, "If the plant has limitations so serious, now is the time to find out. I accept full responsibility."

In the next 30 endless hours, Rickover cut back the Mark I to two-thirds power once and to half-power twice in order to cope with the failing steam pressure, but he never shut it down. Then at 96 hours, the charts in the control room indicated that the submarine had "reached" Ireland. Rickover had taken a terrible chance and he had won. By proving that the *Nautilus* could cross the ocean submerged, he had effectively silenced the opposition to its continued development.

CHAMPAGNE ON HER BOW
From this point on there was clear sailing for the *Nautilus*. The Mark II reactor, a highly refined version of the pioneer Mark I had been built step-by-step in the wake of its predecessor, and, on January 21, 1954, the *Nautilus* was launched. As she slid down the ways into the Thames River at Groton, Connecticut, champagne glistening on her bow, she represented many things to many people: to the world at large, an impressive example of the preëminence of American armed might and technology; to the Navy and the Atomic Energy Commission, an overall investment of something like $250 million; to the engineering profession, a technical masterpiece that had pushed out the frontiers of knowledge in almost every branch of the art; to the men who had produced her, years of unremitting effort, education, and high adventure; to Hyman George Rickover, a goal passionately pursued, finally achieved.

For his pains, Rickover was twice passed over by Navy selection boards for promotion to rear admiral. Under the rules, this would have meant automatic retirement from the service in June, 1953. Congress objected, and through the intervention of the Secretary of the Navy, he was promoted to rear admiral and, in 1958, to vice admiral. President John F. Kennedy intervened in 1961 to prevent Rickover's retirement by the Navy at the required age of sixty-two, and extended his period of active duty for two years. Subsequently, President Lyndon B. Johnson extended his service to 1968.

Still a controversial figure, Vice Admiral Rickover continues to serve as Director of Division Naval Reactors, United States Atomic Energy Commission, and Deputy Commander for Nuclear Propulsion, Naval Ships System Command. He has had the satisfaction of adapting methods used in the Mark I to produce steam for an electricity generating station at Shippingport, Pennsylvania—the world's first industrial nuclear power plant—and he plays an active role in the nation's nuclear submarine program.

Over many years, many people have tried to explain the Navy's unrelenting coldness to Rickover. One veteran Washington reporter summed it up best when he wrote: "The Navy will never forgive him for having forced it to develop the nuclear sub." Forgiven or not, Rickover proved the feasibility of nuclear power for naval propulsion and thereby changed the course of United States naval history, including its engineering, strategy, and personnel training system. But for him, the *Nautilus*—and the whole United States nuclear submarine fleet—might now exist only on a drawing board somewhere in the vast reaches of the Pentagon instead of keeping its critical appointments in the dark waters of the world.

the
xerox
story

IF, A DECADE AGO, a Hollywood screen writer had tried to sell his studio a script about how an impoverished young inventor stumbled upon a fabulous new photographic process, which he patented and offered to many big corporations, all of which turned him down cold; and who then chanced to meet the up-and-coming young president of a conservative old firm who was willing to gamble everything on the process; and how, after agonizing setbacks as well as a streak of dazzling engineering luck, and help from the Army, Navy, and Air Force, the two proceeded to make millions of dollars and create an enterprise with stock worth billions—all in a few years—the chances are that such a writer would have been fired on the spot.

No moviegoer alive, the writer would have been told, would believe such a plot. "Impoverished young inventors" went out with Horatio Alger. Anything resembling a "fabulous new photographic process" would surely have been discovered by Kodak or somebody years ago. Failing that, no "big corporation" worth its salt would have "turned down cold" such a supposedly hot idea. "Conservative old firms" were run by conservative old boards of directors, not by young presidents who "gambled everything" on unheard-of processes. Moreover, "dazzlingly lucky" breaks were scarcely characteristic of modern engineering practice, and a "whole streak" of such coincidences, plus help from the Armed Forces of the United States, was simply intolerable. Last—and most unlikely of all—"millions" in profits and "billions" in stock rolled up in "a few years" taxed credulity right to the breaking point.

If, today, the writer of this offending script were to dig it up, dust it off, and peddle it around again, he might stand an excellent chance of selling it. For now it would be recognized without difficulty as *The Xerox Story*, an outstanding example of a major engineering achievement and of an extremely profitable international business resulting from the efforts of a handful of obscure individuals, not one of whom would qualify as an organization man.

The story of the development of xerography, thus, in truth, closely resembles a movie script, and like the best of them, it comes complete with colorful characters, lucky breaks, suspenseful setbacks, and a denouement right out of M-G-M.

SCENE 1: THE IMPOVERISHED INVENTOR

Chester F. Carlson, at thirty, was the kind of young man who worked all day in the patent department of a large New York electronics firm, went to law school at night, studied on the subway, ate at the Automat, and spent his spare time in the reading room of the Public Library, where he methodically thumbed through technical magazines.

The time was 1935, the middle of the Depression, and Carlson was searching with quiet determination for an idea that might lead to a money-making invention and to a life of less grinding toil and insecurity. He was not groping blindly. For some time, he had noticed that in the office where he worked there never seemed to be enough copies of patent specifications and drawings to go around. Furthermore, there was no convenient way to get them; either a document had to be completely retyped (and proofread) or sent outside for photostatic copying.

Drawing on his physics degree from California Institute of Technology and on boyhood experiments with printing processes, Carlson began to ponder the possibility of inventing an office machine that would take an original document and turn out a perfect copy automatically in a few seconds. Such a machine, he felt sure, would be an extremely desirable convenience for law and engineering firms and all other offices needing quick on-the-spot copies of documents.

There were, of course, various types of office *duplicating* machines already in existence, such as mimeograph and multigraph equipment. These did not work directly from original documents, however, but required intermediate stencils, plates, mats, or other masters which were then used to turn out the number of copies desired. But if the *original* document was to be copied, the only way to do it was to take its picture by Photostat, Rectigraph, or other photographic copying machines consisting of cameras which projected light from the originals onto silver-halide-coated papers (instead of film). Once exposed, the paper then had to be developed as in conventional photography.

The trouble with photographic copying of this type—the situation which had attracted Carlson's attention—was that, since the machines were too costly and space consuming to be installed in most offices, the work to be copied had to be sent to the machines, a time-consuming and inconvenient procedure. Moreover, copies came out white-on-black, required special papers that had to be developed in fixing baths and washed in running water, took approximately 30 minutes apiece to finish, and required the attention of trained operators.

Carlson began to cast about for a solution to these various problems. Knowing that action of light on silver halide had formed the basis for photography ever since Louis Daguerre discovered it in the 1830's, he concluded that time would be wasted in exploring the field further. Instead, he began to look into the effect of light on altogether different substances and, when several pioneering works on photoelectricity fell into his hands, he felt instinctively that he was on the right track. He learned that when light strikes certain types of materials, their electrical conductivity greatly increased. (Sulphur, for instance, had been found to conduct electricity a million times more readily in the light than in the dark.) He also learned that various substances—again, sulphur among them—which were *photoconductors* in the light were *insulators* in the dark, capable of holding an electrical charge for a considerable period of time. Carlson considered the dual nature of these mysterious "photoconductive insulators" for a time, then turned his attention to another, almost equally obscure, branch of electricity, electrostatics.

Known from antiquity as the natural phenomenon whereby certain materials (amber, glass, sulphur, etc.), when rubbed vigorously attract other materials (feathers, lint, hair, etc.), electrostatics had been largely ignored, except in textbooks. No great body of technology based on it had been developed and there were few, if any, electrostatic engineers in the entire electrical profession. Although commanding attention as a nuisance and sometimes a danger in the aircraft, oil, and textile industries, static electricity had found few constructive uses. Nevertheless, Carlson checked back on the basic principle of electrostatics, that objects with the same charge repel each other while objects with opposite charges attract, and, while reviewing the literature on the subject, chanced upon a brief account in a foreign technical review of the recent work of Paul Selenyi, a Hungarian physicist. Selenyi had discovered that images on the end of a cathode ray tube could be developed by dusting the outside of the tube face with a positively charged powder such as lycopodium, a fine, symmetrically-grained substance composed of the spores of club moss. The powder would adhere to the tube at the places where negative electrostatic charges had been deposited on the inside by the electron scanning beam. The powder image could then be removed from the tube by pressing treated paper against it.

SCENE 2: FABULOUS NEW PHOTO PROCESS

At this point in his search, Carlson began to juxtapose what he knew of photoconductive insulators with what he knew of electrostatics. He then asked himself a critical question: What would happen if a charge of static electricity were given to a photoconductive insulator, such as sulphur-coated plate, by rubbing it vigorously in the dark then exposing it to a pattern of light in such a way that some areas of the plate were illuminated and other areas kept in darkness? If his guess was right, the electrostatic charge on the illuminated areas would be lost through photoconductivity while the charge on the unilluminated areas would be retained through photoinsulation.

This intriguing conclusion led to another question: What if the pattern of light on the plate could be created by shining a lamp onto it *through a typewritten sheet of paper?* Theoretically, the pattern of white background and dark type of the sheet should be re-created on the plate in the form of absence and presence of electrostatic charges. If this electrostatic image were then dusted with some dark powder, such as dyed lycopodium, which had been given a charge opposite in polarity to that on the plate, the powder should adhere to the charged areas— representing the type—through electrostatic attraction. If so, there should then appear a reverse-reading powder image on the surface of the plate. It would only remain to transfer this powder image by pressing against it a sheet of paper with a slightly adhesive surface. The result? A black-on-white, right-reading copy of an original document made completely free of chemicals, fixing baths, and all the expensive paraphernalia of conventional photography.

Elated by the thought that he had struck upon an idea which might solve the document-copying problem, Carlson, in October, 1937, put his newly-gained knowledge of patent law to work and filed a preliminary application covering the basic process, which he called "electro-photography." He then began to tackle the formidable job of trying to make his idea work.

It was fortunate for Carlson that he could not foresee the assorted pitfalls, blind alleys, land mines, and other hazards that lay ahead. Using as a laboratory, first the closet of his apartment in Jackson Heights, then a second-floor room behind a beauty parlor in Astoria, Long Island, he experimented doggedly for months with photoconductive materials, plate metals, and developing powders before finally achieving his first electrophotograph in October, 1938. It was a primitive affair. Using a sulphur-coated zinc plate and a glass microscope slide on which "10-22-38 ASTORIA" had been printed in India ink, Carlson rubbed the surface of the plate with a handkerchief to apply the electrostatic charge. He then placed the slide on the plate and shone a floodlamp through it for a few seconds. Removing the slide, he dusted the plate below with lycopodium powder, blew off the loose grains, and saw—to his gratification—a near-perfect image in powder of the legend on the slide. He then pressed wax paper to the powder image, heated the paper· to "fix" the powder on it and held in his hand the world's first electrophotograph.

Fully aware that this simple procedure would be highly unimpressive to potential backers, Carlson set about to design equipment which he could use to demonstrate his process, and by the middle of the next year he had developed a machine which used a drum instead of a flat plate to provide the photoconductive

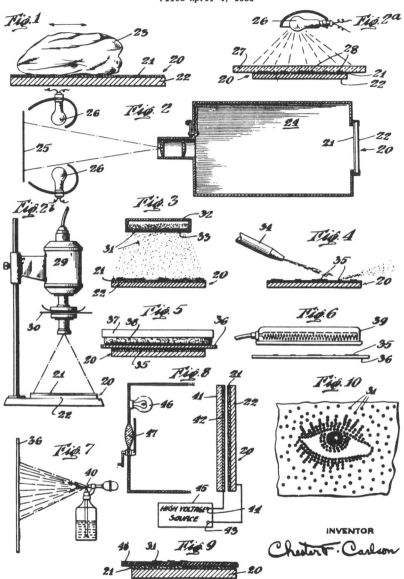

INVENTOR

Chester F. Carlson

Drawings from the patent application

surface. Covered with aluminum foil coated with anthracene, a photoconductive insulator, the surface of the drum was given an electrostatic charge by passing a plush belt, mounted on rollers, around it at high speed. The document to be copied—on translucent paper—was placed directly on the drum surface and an incandescent light shone onto it. The document was then removed and the drum surface dusted by means of a rotating bristle brush with powdered resin pigmented with carbon black. A sheet of dampened paper was then pressed by a rubber roller against the powder image to produce a copy.

SCENE 3: TURNED DOWN COLD
Although not completely satisfied with this machine, Carlson applied for patents on it, and in 1940 began an intensive effort to enlist commercial support for the invention. In the next few years, he approached more than 20 companies, among them International Business Machines Corporation, Remington Rand Corporation, the Charles Bruning Company, American Type Founders, Research Corporation, and Kollsman Instruments Company, as well as the Army Signal Corps and the National Inventors Council. None was impressed. Reactions ranged from comments that the invention was "crude" and "toylike" to "bizarre" and "ridiculous." When the disruptions of World War II contributed still further to what Carlson called the "enthusiastic lack of interest" in his process, he faced the gloomy prospect that the value of his basic patents, granted in 1940 and 1942 and with seventeen years to run, would be progressively eroded by further substantial delay.

Then in 1944, while on a visit to Battelle Memorial Institute, a non-profit industrial research organization in Columbus, Ohio, in connection with an assignment for his employer, Carlson described his invention to a Battelle engineer, who invited Carlson to give a demonstration. When it subsequently appeared that Carlson's work fitted in admirably with a new department created by Battelle to explore industrial developments in the graphic arts, an agreement was reached whereby Battelle would undertake development work of the process in exchange for exclusive rights to Carlson's patents and 60 per cent of any proceeds from them. Carlson was to receive the remaining 40 per cent of the proceeds from the licensing of Carlson and Battelle patents.

Had such a speculative, open-end agreement been contracted with a less aggressive and skilled engineering organization than Battelle, it might have proved a disastrous move by Carlson. But Battelle meant business. Although aware that every aspect of Carlson's invention stemmed from largely unexplored, "twilight" areas of electrical phenomena, Battelle engineers began work in October, 1944, in makeshift space above a foundry in Columbus, to explore photoconductive insulator materials, methods of surface electrical charging, materials for developing powders, and the mechanics of transferring powder images to paper.

Meantime, Carlson's fortunes received a boost from another quarter. In the summer of 1944, an article on his electrophotographic process had appeared in a technical publication.* It aroused little interest until a full year later when an abstract of it came across the desk of Dr. John H. Dessauer, director of the small technical staff of the Haloid Company of Rochester, New York. Haloid was a minor producer of photocopying machines, photographic papers and supplies with which the giant Eastman Kodak Company—one eye on the Department of Justice's Anti-Trust Division—was happy to compete. Dessauer recalls, "It was as if lightning had struck when I read that article. It seemed to me that Carlson's process had distinct commercial possibilities for reproducing documents and letters—and this was a field in which Haloid had been increasingly interested for some time." He lost no time in recommending to his boss, Joseph C. Wilson, vice-president of Haloid, that the company

* *Radio News* (now *Electronics World*), July, 1944.

get in touch with Carlson immediately with an eye to investigating the process further.

Joe Wilson, thirty-six and eleven years out of Harvard Business School, was beginning to worry about both his own future and that of the Haloid Company. Although the firm had enjoyed a regular—but strictly circumscribed—prosperity since 1906, the sagging prices of photographic supplies and the rising costs of labor and materials after World War II had cut substantially into the company's profits. To Wilson it seemed imperative to strike out in some new direction, a point of view not shared by a few older members of the management. He was in a receptive mood, therefore, to Dessauer's recommendation. As Haloid was too strapped financially to pay for a special mission to see Carlson, he called on an associate in New York to do so and soon learned that Carlson had concluded a deal with Battelle Memorial Institute. Wilson, now chairman of the board of Haloid, decided to go to Columbus with Dessauer to look into the invention.

Despite several improvements by Battelle engineers, Carlson's process was still extremely crude and Wilson was full of misgivings when he saw it, but he decided to take a chance on it anyway. Early in 1947, he signed a cautious agreement to underwrite Battelle's developmental work to the extent of $10,000 a year in exchange for a limited license to use the process in making office copying machines. A year later, he obtained exclusive rights for that purpose in exchange for a commitment to pay substantial royalties to Battelle.

During the next few years, everyone connected with Carlson's process lived in the supercharged atmosphere of a high-stakes poker game. To the consternation of Haloid's stockholders, Wilson bet all the company's earnings from its regular products and another $3.5 million raised through loans and stock issues on electrophotography. Backing the gamble with stock purchases out of personal resources, Wilson threw into the pot all his savings and whatever he could borrow, while Dessauer further upped the ante with everything he owned but his life insurance policy. Carlson, as part of his agreement with Battelle, staked all his meagre savings as well as funds borrowed from friends in order to keep his 40 per cent equity from shrinking to 25 per cent. To conserve cash, Haloid even paid off some of its large creditors with shares of stock. Recalling these hectic early days, Dessauer says, "With one crisis following another, a panicky boss could easily have lost his mind. But Joe always remained calm—and now, he finally had the confidence of the board of directors. That made a big difference." Just how big no one could have possibly envisioned.

SCENE 5: A STREAK OF DAZZLING LUCK
As the engineers at Battelle Memorial Institute continued to experiment with Carlson's electrophotographic machine model, their goal became to convert it from its limited state as a "contact" exposure device—in which the document to be copied had to be on translucent paper, printed on one side only, so that light could shine through it *directly* onto the plate—into a form of camera in which the document could be exposed behind a lens and light from it *projected* onto the plate. In the latter situation, the document could be printed on any kind of paper and its reverse side could be copied by simply turning it over. There was one formidable obstacle, however: the sulphur or anthracene-coated plates and drums used by Carlson reacted too slowly to light to make exposure behind a lens practical. What was needed was a much faster, more sensitive photoconductive material.

To find such a material, the Battelle group began to experiment with mixtures of sulphur and various other light-sensitive substances, among them the element selenium. They began by adding 5 per cent selenium to the sulphur and, when some improvement resulted, gradually increased the proportion to 20 per cent, 50 per cent, and 95 per cent. At this point they decided to try a plate coated with 100 per cent selenium. One of the engineers recalls the experiment:

> We pulled down the shades in the lab just the way we always did when we put a charge on a plate, then we exposed this new plate to a document in the usual way and checked to see if we were getting any images. We couldn't find a damn thing and were just about to decide that pure selenium wouldn't work when somebody said, "Maybe there's too much light in the room. Let's try it again in real darkness." So we did and there on the plate were the most beautiful images we'd ever had. And just think, we almost missed it!

With the discovery of pure selenium as a highly efficient photoconductive insulator with maximum sensitivity in the blue-ultraviolet region of the spectrum, it now became possible for the Battelle group to plan a camera in which fluorescent light, shone onto a document through a lens, could be projected onto a metal plate coated with a thin film of selenium to produce well-defined images at about the same speed and with the same sharpness as the silver halide process. But there was one hitch. Experimental selenium-coated plates had been made in the laboratory, but no technology existed for producing them in quantity. As a matter of fact, selenium exhibited widely different characteristics in its crystalline, metallic, and vitreous forms, and not much was known about how it behaved in any of them. Then a Haloid engineer discovered that vitreous selenium evaporated under high vacuum could be deposited on aluminum or brass in successive layers to produce uniform coatings as thin as 30 to 50 microns (one- to two-thousandths of an inch).

The excitement created by the breakthroughs with selenium brought about developments in all phases of Battelle's work on electrophotography. To replace the awkward plush belt used by Carlson to put a charge of static electricity on the photo-conductive plate, one of the engineers invented a method of applying charge by means of a "corona emission" device. He had started with the knowledge that if a sufficiently high voltage was applied to a wire parallel to a photoconductive insulator, air around the wire would become ionized and the ions with a charge the same as that on the wire would be swept across to the insulating surface. If this "corona current," which appeared as a bluish-white glow all along the wire, was maintained, it would literally spray ions over the insulating surface of the parallel plate. However, there was no known way to control the corona current so that the charge would be evenly distributed on the plate and held at constant voltage—imperative to prevent overcharging and damaging of the sensitive plate. To accomplish this, another engineer came up with the idea of placing a third element in the form of a control screen between the wire and the parallel plate. Serving somewhat the same purpose as the grid between the cathode and plate of a vacuum tube, the screen would carry an electrical potential sufficient to enable it to control the ion flow to the surface of the plate by regulating the electric field between the corona wire and the plate.

This device proved highly satisfactory and led to an equally important development at the opposite end of the process: the transfer of the powder-developed image from the photoconductive plate to the copy paper. In Carlson's original machine, this transfer had been accomplished by pressing treated paper directly onto the powder image. It now occurred to still another Battelle engineer that here, too, corona emission could be employed to do the job, thereby making it possible to create copies on ordinary, untreated paper. He did this by placing the paper over the powder image and spraying over the back of the sheet a corona current with a polarity opposite to that of the charged powder particles on the photoconductive surface. Through static attraction, the particles would then leave the surface of the photoconductor and adhere to the paper. The sheet could then be pulled off and the powder fused permanently on it through heat.

As one engineering success followed another, there remained one area of Carlson's process which defiantly resisted improvement. Regardless of the type of developer powder used to bring out the electrostatic image on the photoconductive plate (lycopodium had been succeeded by natural resins and plastics of various kinds pigmented with carbon black), thorny problems remained. When the powder was dusted over the plate, particles adhered not only to the image but to the background areas as well, producing a grey, smudged appearance. Some particles clumped together, creating black spots that blanked out words or made them illegible. In an effort to obtain a cleaner background, one of the Battelle group tried mixing relatively coarse, granular ammonium chloride with the developer powder on the theory that the heavier salt particles would sweep the background clean.

They did, but for a completely unforeseen reason. It had happened—quite by accident—that ammonium chloride, in frictional contact with the powder, picked up a static charge opposite to that of the powder and the same as that of the plate. The salt and the plate thus competed for the powder, with the result that on the image portions of the plate where the electrostatic charge was strong (the dark areas), the image captured the powder, while on the background portions, which had lost their charge, the salt captured the powder and swept it away. This obscure phenomenon, known as the "triboelectric effect," set Battelle off on the most comprehensive study of the effect ever made to establish which charge, negative or positive, various materials acquire when exposed to friction with others. Financed by Haloid, the study covered hundreds of materials, continued for years, and supplied findings which made it possible to create greatly improved developing mixtures composed of two elements: granular "carrier" substances such as tiny glass, plastic, or sand beads, and pigmented "toner" powders. Combinations of these elements were chosen on the basis of their ability to induce opposite charges of static electricity in each other when rubbed together. A mechanical method of developing the plate by placing it in a wooden tray and cascading the powder back and forth over it—in a manner reminiscent of panning for gold—was then worked out.

By the fall of 1948, Battelle and Haloid were convinced that Carlson's electrophotographic process, which they had renamed "xerography," was ready to make its public debut.* On October 22, ten years to the day since Carlson had made his first picture in Astoria, the "bread-board" model put together by Battelle was demonstrated in Detroit before a meeting of the Optical Society of America. More than a thousand physicists, engineers, optical experts, and science writers watched in absorbed silence as a line drawing of Benjamin Franklin was put into the camera at one end of the machine and, a few minutes later, a clear copy of it removed from the wooden developing tray at the other end. The message was not lost on the distinguished audience. As one publication noted later: "A photograph has for over 100 years meant only one thing—an image formed by the action of light on certain silver salts. This long monopoly of silver chemistry has now been broken by xerography."

SCENE 6: AGONIZING SETBACKS
While the Detroit demonstration took xerography out of the obscurity in which it had been sunk for ten years, it also revealed unmistakably that a commercial photocopying machine based on the art was a long way off. In mid-1948, Haloid

* From the Greek words *"xerox"* (dry) and *"graphos"* (writing), to emphasize the contrast with wet chemical photography.

began to supplement the work going on at Battelle with efforts of its own, carried on in an old house on a back street in Rochester. At that time, there were only 15 people in the company's research department. Engineers knowledgeable in the fields of photoelectricity and electrostatics were impossible to find, and the firm's finances were at a low ebb. Dessauer nevertheless managed to organize a team to work on xerography, with Dr. Harold Clark heading a group to investigate the basic physics of selenium, developer materials, and other essential elements of the process—still largely a scientific no-man's land— and Clyde Mayo leading a group to develop the hardware to be used in an office copier.

Recalling these first beginnings, Clark points out, "As we tried to get solid-state physicists to join us, we realized that self-respecting scientists were most uneasy about staking their futures on a study of such a wild material as selenium." For Mayo, the problem was different but equally frustrating. "There stood xerography, producing good images on occasion and failing at other times for reasons that we did not understand. Yet we had to try to develop reliability of the process to the point where it could be used in a machine that was both automatic and automated."

Despite the misgivings of nearly everybody, economic necessity led the Haloid management to put a xerographic machine on the market in 1950 in the form of a Xerox Copier, a manually-operated machine based on the Battelle bread-board model. As a copying device, it was a flop. Since the copier employed direct contact exposure of the selenium plate to light, instead of exposure behind a lens, only translucent originals printed on one side could be handled. The developer powder, which was applied in a tray arrangement and transferred to copy paper by corona discharge, was fixed on the paper in another separate operation involving a hot plate. In all, some 18 to 19 manipulations were required to make each copy. Finally—and disastrously—a soybean meal preparation, used to clean the plate of powder before reuse, proved to be highly susceptible to humidity. When the first Xerox Copiers went out in the summer of 1950, the hygroscopic meal left dampness on the selenium plates and ruined their surfaces. Documents went into one end of the machine—blank paper came out the other end.

In the ruckus that ensued, equipment began to come back, customers refused to pay, and word began to get around that the Xerox machines were a failure. Some Haloid stockholders—to their everlasting regret—rushed to sell their shares. Wilson, meantime, refused to panic. After ordering a crash program to determine what had gone wrong and how to fix it, he replaced all the damaged plates, substituted a more suitable material for the offending soybean meal, and took stock of the situation. Clearly, the Xerox Copier was a failure as an office copier. However, some time before the humidity problem developed, Battelle engineers had discovered that the developer "toner" powders used in the process had unexpectedly proved to be excellent ink receptors, with the result that paper off-set masters for use in lithographic machines could be made on the Xerox equipment for much less than they usually cost.*

Wilson, grasping at this straw, decided to go after the lithographic market. He converted the Xerox Copier into the Xerox LithMaster Processor, equipped it with camera-type exposure and in 1951 began to *lease* the machine to offices employing lithograph and other duplicating equipment for use in making masters. The strategy quickly paid off. Competitive methods of preparing off-set masters cost about $1.65 a page, while the Xerox machine could do the job for about $.30 a page, including the rental fee. Soon, Haloid had carved out a very profitable market for itself. "The move really saved the day in our first round," says Dessauer.

* A paper off-set master is chemically treated in such a way that when the surface is inked, only certain parts will absorb the ink and print.

Scene 7: army, navy, and air force

By 1953, Haloid began to see clear sailing ahead for the first time since Wilson took his fateful trip to Columbus in 1946. While part of the company's improved financial health was due to the success of the LithMaster Processor, an equally important part was attributable to the sudden interest in xerography on the part of the armed services. Both the Navy and the Air Force realized that time and money could be saved if engineering drawings, specification sheets, and other complex original documents could be microfilmed, then subsequently enlarged and photocopied on ordinary paper by the xerographic process. The Army Signal Corps was interested for another reason: unlike silver halide photography, xerographic materials were not damaged and the process was not inhibited by the nuclear radiation that might be encountered in an atomic war.

Working under government contracts, Haloid between 1950 and 1960 developed several large, institutional-type machines for enlarging microfilm images and making xerographic prints of them. Copyflo 11, a machine capable of reproducing from rolls of either 16mm. or 35mm. microfilm, turned out prints on a continuous web of paper at the rate of 20 feet a minute. A very special machine, the Copyflo 24, was designed for the Navy to produce copies in volume of engineering drawings enlarged from microfilm at the rate of a 24- by 36-inch print every 10 seconds. There was one very significant feature in both the Copyflo 11 and 24: for the first time since Carlson's early demonstration model, a rotary drum was used for the photoconductive surface instead of a flat plate.

The return to the drum proved to be the key to the automation of the xerographic process, for it made possible the arrangement of the various process steps at stationary locations around the periphery of the rotating cylinder, so that each step could be carried out sequentially on different parts of the surface. While one part was exposed, another part was developed with powder, another part involved in electrostatic transfer, and still another part cleaned for re-exposure. Profiting from the invaluable experience with automation gained in their work with the Copyflo machines, Haloid's research and engineering group went all out to develop a selenium-coated drum which could be used as the heart of a smaller high-speed office copier.

This proved to be no easy task. If the drum size was reduced too greatly, while the scanning speed of two inches-per-second was maintained, the quality of the images was damaged. Moreover, experiments indicated that better performance might result if the original document was held stationary and a moving lens used (instead of a moving document and a stationary lens), even though a moving lens meant larger, more complicated equipment. It gradually became clear, as efforts to miniaturize the components proceeded, that not only was a "desk-top" size machine then impractical, but that if a copier was to be *truly* automatic, reliable, easily serviced, and capable of high quality performance in the hands of unskilled personnel, it would have to be about the size of a four-drawer filing cabinet, weigh 400 to 800 pounds, and cost around $2,000. This news caused sharp depression among the Haloid management. Three different marketing research organizations had warned the company that investigations showed unmistakably that a big, expensive machine would never survive the competition with all the smaller, cheaper office copying devices on the market. Yet it was the very nature of the xerographic process that all the steps must be carried on in one spot—unlike the ordinary photographic copying process in which most of the developing was done outside the machine. Then just as hopes of penetrating the lucrative office copier market began to glimmer, Haloid enjoyed yet another warm embrace by the long arm of coincidence.

One of the company's crew of bright, young field representatives had noticed, while making sales calls, that office copiers of every type routinely occupied the entire top of either an office desk or a large table from which they were rarely moved. He concluded that small size and light weight were not such vital factors after all, but that convenient operation, reliable, trouble-free service, and production of excellent copies on ordinary paper were the overriding considerations. He passed this shrewd observation along to headquarters in Rochester and thereby altered the destiny of the company. Those members of the management who favored continuation of the development of the 914 Office Copier now were able to swing the decision their way.* Engineering efforts to produce a machine unhampered by considerations of size and cost were redoubled and by 1957, a bread-board model was completed.

Although much of the basic technology of the 914 had been evolved at Battelle and Haloid in the course of the work on the LithMaster and Copyflo machines, some important new features were added by research and by Clyde Mayo and his engineering group. A glass platen arrangement for exposing the object to be copied was developed which proved to be so flexible that even bulky objects such as books and packages could be handled easily. While these objects remained stationary, a moving lens device scanned their surfaces, projecting moving images in synchronization with the rotating selenium-coated drum. By an ingenious arrangement of mirrors, a folded optical path was created which helped to reduce the space required for the moving lens assembly. In another, earlier development, to sharpen the images on the photoconductive surface, the 914's 8-inch aluminum drum was given a coating of aluminum oxide *before* selenium was deposited on the surface in order to prevent free

* The machine was named for the maximum copy-size of 9 inches by 14 inches.

electrons from the aluminum substratum from penetrating to the top and trapping positive ions there. An arrangement was also worked out to control the corona current more exactly in the electrostatic charging of the drum. A device called a "corotron" was invented to shield the corona wires in such a way that they could safely carry much higher voltages without overcharging and damaging the drum surface. Replacing the continuous paper rolls used on the Copyflo machines, a feed-in system for individual sheets was provided, and—to prevent the pages from adhering to the drum—a technique was worked out to blow the leading edge of the page off the drum by air jets. Finally, automatic controls were devised making it possible to produce the number of copies desired at the push of a button. Here—at last —was Carlson's original dream realized.

As the engineering model of the 914 neared completion, Haloid found itself facing a major decision. Should some other company be licensed to manufacture and sell the copier, with Haloid settling for royalty payments? Or should the little firm risk everything by taking on the manufacturing and sales job itself? Many in the company felt that its lack of large-scale manufacturing facilities, marketing resources, and manpower added up to insuperable obstacles. It was decided to negotiate with International Business Machines Corporation on the matter of an exclusive license to build the 914.

Fortunately for Haloid, IBM for the second time turned down a chance to get into xerography. And now Wilson called into play both his business genius and his very considerable powers of persuasion. He suggested to the doubting Thomases in the management that any lingering reservations about whether the 914 would sell or not could be put to rest by not selling it at all. Haloid would lease it instead, as had been done so successfully with the LithMaster Processor, and charge a fee per copy through a meter arrangement. "With the decision to go ahead with the 914," says Dessauer, "we took a risk of a magnitude that can best be described by saying that we bet our whole company at that time. Our judgment paid off."

SCENE 8: MILLIONS AND BILLIONS

The Xerox 914 Office Copier hit the market in March, 1960, and it touched off a sweeping revolution in the history of office machinery. Renting for $95 a month, with no charge for the first 2,000 copies and additional copies for $.035 each, the 914 quickly overwhelmed smaller copying machines which sold for $100 to $500 and averaged anywhere from $.05 to $.085 per copy in costs of the special papers and chemicals required. While the lower cost per copy was one reason for the 914's success, another soon became clear. Previously unremarked, an aversion among secretaries and other office personnel to the "messy chemicals" involved in the wet processes had been building to sizeable proportions. In contrast, the Xerox machine with its *completely dry* process, producing permanent copies on *ordinary* paper, was irresistible. Moreover, the flexibility and convenience of the machine were equally attractive. Anywhere from one to 15 copies, or a continuous flow, could be produced by pressing a button, with the first copy requiring only 30 seconds to make and additional copies 8 seconds each. There was no limit to what could be copied—from newspaper clippings and handwritten letters to three-dimensional objects.

By the end of 1960, as secretaries from coast to coast nagged their bosses to get rid of wet process copiers and substitute 914's, Xerox Corporation had leased 2,000 of the machines (twice its rosiest expectations) and within five years the figure had risen to 60,000.* From 1959, the year before introducing the 914, when Haloid's sales were $33 million, the total grew to $480 million

* Haloid Company, after acquiring all patents relating to xerography from Battelle in 1956, became Haloid-Xerox Corporation and changed its name to Xerox Corporation in 1960.

by the middle of the 1960's. Underlying these impressive figures was a solid economic fact: while each 914 cost about $2,000, it returned an average of $4,500 *yearly* in fees and rentals to Xerox. As a result of all this prosperity, Xerox stockholders experienced a veritable transport of equity increase. Haloid stock, which could have been bought in 1957 for as little as $1.80 a share, reached a high of $267 in 1966.* By the mid-1960's the value of the company's outstanding stock amounted to nearly $5.5 billion—more than that of United States Steel and Bethlehem Steel combined. Meantime, Battelle Memorial Institute, under its arrangement with Xerox, garnered a total of $425 million in cash and stock payments, and Chester Carlson, under his arrangement with Battelle, realized upwards of $25 million. Even the residents of Rochester shared in the euphoria as Xerox manufacturing operations expanded overnight to keep up with the growing backlog of orders for 914's. The University of Rochester, with an original investment in Haloid stock of $196,000, saw its equity grow to $100,000,000. In the words of one observer, "To the people of Rochester, Xerox has been something like the Second Coming of Kodak."

Although Wilson and his engineering team were surprised and gratified by the remarkable success of the 914, their feelings resembled those of an expectant father whose wife presents him with triplets. "Our whole way of life was changed almost overnight," says one of the group somewhat wistfully. High up on the list of the changes was a major expansion in the Research and Engineering division's budget. It soon became routine for approximately 8 to 9 per cent of the company's annual revenue to be devoted to Research and Engineering with about one-tenth of this going for fundamental work in solid-state physics, chemistry of solids, gaseous electronics, and electrostatics, and two-thirds going into product development work. The Research and Engineering division grew rapidly from Dessauer's original 15

---

* Since 1948, the company's stock has split 60 times.

pioneers to 900 physicists and electro-mechanical engineers, about 100 of whom held doctoral degrees, 150 masters' and over 600 bachelors' degrees.

The investment in talent soon paid off in other profitable Xerox products. In 1963, the long-sought goal of a desk-top copier was achieved in the 813 model—the first Xerox product developed without the support of government funds. Engineered for Xerox from concepts originally developed in the laboratories of Battelle Memorial Institute, the 813 was designed for smaller offices requiring fewer copies than 914 users. A less versatile machine than its predecessor, the 813 was based on a "moving document-stationary lens" system which restricted the input material to routine business papers. Then in 1965, Xerox unveiled its *pièce de résistance,* the 2400 Copier, the culmination of five years of engineering effort and the highest speed photocopying device ever made. Turning out 2,400 copies hourly (one every one and a half seconds) its speed began to approximate that of duplicating machines and even printing processes. Engineered to give high quality performance over long periods of time with minimal wear and tear, the 2400 machines were expected to reduce maintenance calls—a costly service to Xerox —by a factor of ten. Toward this end, the moving lens assembly of the 914 was replaced in the 2400 by an oscillating mirror and stationary lens, the paper feed was improved, and the fusing of the developer power on the copies was accomplished by a combination of heat and pressure instead of by the less efficient process of heat alone.

The work of the Xerox Research and Engineering division has gone into fields far beyond the limited area of product development, however. As the first commercial application of xerography, the office copiers, while representing a triumphant combination of engineering skill and business acumen, barely brushed the surface of the potential of xerography. Still ahead are such exciting applications as Long Distance Xerography

(LDX), combining xerography with facsimile to transmit images by wire or microwave across thousands of miles; xerographic printers capable of taking computer (or radar) output and translating it into numbers, letters, diagrams, and drawings; xerographic information retrieval systems for libraries; and the use of xerographic techniques to reproduce printed microminiature circuits. On all of these fronts, Xerox engineers are working diligently—often beyond a wall of secrecy for reasons both of security and of proprietary interest.*

SCENE 9: EPILOGUE

What accounts for Xerox's success? What were the separate factors which, added together, yielded such an unexpected total? Lewis E. Walkup, a member of Battelle Memorial Institute and a major patent-holder and contributor to the development of xerography, has some ideas on the subject. First of all, he points out, photoconductivity in insulators and electrostatics were areas in which virtually nobody else was interested. Carlson's invention was, actually, a perfect example of the off-beat idea that rarely comes out of the vast laboratories of big corporations. Secondly, even after xerography was publicly unveiled in 1948, Haloid was left pretty much alone by the competition in the ten years between the failure of its first office copier and the success of its second—a grace period not usually enjoyed by companies in competitive businesses. Most importantly, nobody realized the growing need among companies—large and small—for multiple copies of documents, or that such firms would be willing to pay a nickel a copy to get them. Says Walkup, "If we who were associated with the development had tried to estimate the potential market for copiers in the laboratories, we would have

---

* The last of Carlson's original patents on xerography expired in 1961. However, each of the secondary patents amassed on technical improvements, new applications, etc., has extended the company's protection another seventeen years.

multiplied the current photocopy market by five or so just to be optimistic—and would have underestimated the real potential market by *thousands* of times."

Dr. John Dessauer makes the same point more philosophically. "Sometimes it occurs to me," he says thoughtfully, "that invention is really the mother of necessity."

the
tooth
of time

Samuel f. b. morse invented the electric telegraph in 1832, and in 1858 the first submarine telegraph cable was put down between North America and Great Britain. Alexander Graham Bell invented the telephone in 1876, but it was not until 1956 that a transatlantic telephone cable linked the two places.

In the century that elapsed between the laying of the two cables, most of the history of United States communications was written. To review this history, however, is to do more than reflect upon a hundred years of technical progress. Rather, it is to highlight the fact that true technical progress cannot be achieved to any lasting degree except through true technical competence. This proposition may seem to be almost axiomatic, yet the story of the two cables is essentially a study in contrast between the technical competence of those involved in the two huge projects. As such, it serves to remind us that vast disparities in engineering technique and responsibility continue to exist today—as evidenced by occasional, spectacular failures such as the "Sugar

Grove" radio telescope, Project Mohole, and the Ranger un
manned spacecraft moon exploration program.* But although
the goal of consistent engineering excellence still eludes us, the
determined search for it nevertheless continues.

THE SHORTER ROAD TO WEALTH

In the early 1830's while Morse was feverishly working on the
telegraph in a cluttered machine shop in New Haven, Connecticut, the tide of invention in the United States was building
toward flood point. Under the spell of quick fortunes to be made,
farmhands, artists, college professors, small businessmen—all
strove to add to the stream of mechanical contrivances that
poured onto receptive markets both at home and abroad.

Often, success was cruelly elusive. Morse, once a successful
portrait painter and sculptor, was obliged to languish in poverty
for years, despite his invention, until recognition came. Morse
had first become interested in electromagnetism as a result of
important discoveries made in the field during the 1820's. After
the Danish physicist, Hans Christian Oersted, had established
that an electric current flowing through a wire creates a magnetic field around it, two experimenters, William Sturgeon in
England and Joseph Henry in the United States, found that an
iron core surrounded by an electrical coil could be magnetized
by making and breaking the electrical circuits. It remained for
Morse—with considerable help from his assistant, Alfred Vail,
and from Henry himself—to hit on the manner in which the
electromagnet could be adapted to create an electric telegraph.
By the middle of the 1830's he had fully demonstrated not only
that a magnet could be employed to detect the making and

---

* The Sugar Grove project to build the world's largest radio telescope
was cancelled as impractical after six years and $63 million had been
spent on it; Project Mohole, calling for a hole to be drilled deep into the
earth's mantle for geological investigation, was abandoned after its costs
ballooned over 1000 per cent; the Ranger program between 1961 and
1964 chalked up six failures in six tries.

breaking of an electrical circuit but that it could be done in a coded pattern and in such a way as to transmit intelligence over long distances. Nevertheless, it was not until 1843 that he succeeded in persuading Congress to vote money for an experimental telegraph line between Washington and Baltimore. Then, almost overnight, his name and fame were "made"—in true nineteenth-century fashion.

To span the gap

The electric telegraph was the first important practical application of electricity and one of the most financially successful inventions of all time. Within a few years after its introduction, a network of telegraph wires reached up and down the Atlantic seaboard and penetrated west along the roadbeds of the nation's rapidly expanding rail lines. On the other side of the Atlantic, two British inventors, W. F. Cooke and Charles Wheatstone, had produced an electric telegraph along somewhat different lines from that of Morse, and, by 1850, a telegraph system linked all the major cities of England. From that point on, it was inevitable that adventurous entrepreneurs on both sides of the Atlantic should be fired by the idea of spanning the 2,500-mile gap between the two countries by ocean cable, thereby cutting the time required to transmit intelligence from four weeks to a few minutes.

The technical feasibility of such a scheme rested on somewhat dubious evidence. Morse himself, in 1842, had put down an insulated wire beneath the East River in New York to test the practicality of underwater telegraphy, and on the basis of these experiments had notified the United States Government that a transatlantic telegraph cable was technically possible. A few years earlier, Wheatstone had proposed to the House of Commons that a telegraph cable be put down between England and France across the Strait of Dover. However, it was not until 1850 that a cable was laid beneath the English Channel at its narrowest point between Dover and Cape Gris-Nez on the French coast.* This was followed in quick succession by underwater links in various parts of the world, and, by the middle of the decade, the British, despite several spectacular and costly failures due to inexperience in cable design and laying, had established themselves as leaders in the thriving submarine cable business.

In each of these installations, however, the waters involved were relatively shallow and the distances to be traversed were short. Largely unexplored were such basic considerations for a transatlantic cable as the character of the ocean floor, the diminution of signal strength in long-distance underwater transmission, and the technique of laying cable at great ocean depths. Some mathematicians stated flatly that it was *not possible* to submerge a cable at ocean depths and that, even if it were, no signals could be sent over such a great distance.

ENTER MR. FIELD

Onto this crowded stage came a practical man who determined to resolve the question of the feasibility of the transatlantic cable. Cyrus W. Field, a successful New York merchant, had become interested in the idea of the cable after meeting a British engineer who was trying to raise money to complete a land telegraph line across Newfoundland and hook it up with a submarine cable to Nova Scotia. Speculating that such a scheme could mean connecting New York by cable to a point a thousand miles to the east, Field became intrigued by the prospect of continuing the line on across the Atlantic.

Aware of the vital scientific questions that remained to be answered, Field requested an opinion from a leading ocea-

---

* Unfortunately, a French fisherman caught the cable with his anchor the day after it began operating. On hauling it to the surface, he decided it was a strange form of seaweed and briskly chopped it in two—an act which presaged generations of warfare between cable owners and fishermen.

nographer, and—to set his mind at rest on electrical matters—
he sought advice from Morse. Not surprisingly, the latter en-
thusiastically supported the plan, citing his experiments in New
York harbor eleven years earlier. The report from the ocea-
nographer was somewhat more guarded. "It is an established
fact," he wrote weightily, "that there is no running water at
the bottom of the deep sea.* The agents which disturb the
equilibrium of the sea, giving violence to its waves and force to
its currents, all reside near or above its surface, none of them
have their home in its depths." He concluded that a deep sea
cable "would lie in cold obstruction, without anything to fret,
chafe or wear, *save alone the tooth of time*." However, he
cautioned, "I do not pretend to consider the question as to the
possibility of finding a time calm enough, the sea smooth
enough, a wire long enough, or a ship big enough to lay a coil
of wire sixteen hundred miles in length."

Prophetic words. But Field was a sanguine man, of bound-
less faith and energy. He set about at once to obtain a charter
from the Newfoundland government and to raise money to complete the telegraph system between Newfoundland and Nova
Scotia. By the middle of 1856, the telegraph system stretched
imposingly from New York to St. John's, the capital of Newfoundland.

Now that the time had come to add the all-important transoceanic link, Field went to England and appealed to the Government as well as to private capital for financial support. Within
two months, the persuasive American had obtained not only a
government subsidy, plus the promise of a British ship to help
lay the cable, but had formed the Atlantic Telegraph Company
with $2.5 million of private capital subscribed by such eminent
Victorians as William Makepeace Thackeray and Lady Byron.

---

* It was not until the twentieth century that the occurrence of turbidity
currents at great sea depths was discovered.

Equally important to Field was the backing of Professor William Thomson,* of the University of Glasgow, a physicist and mathematician who was to bridge the gap between the theoretical problems of submarine cables and their actual installation and operation. Thomson not only believed in the scientific feasibility of the cable, but also agreed to become a director of the newly-formed company and eventually served as on-board electrician during the early cable laying expeditions. He invented an essential new instrument, the marine galvanometer, which was to contribute heavily to the ultimate success of the transatlantic telegraph cable by increasing the capacity of receiving equipment from two words to twenty words a minute. His thoughtful, scholarly approach to telegraphy effectively complemented the promotional genius of Field.

To try men's souls

Eager to get the submarine cable working during the summer of 1857, the directors of the Atlantic Telegraph Company placed orders with two British cable companies to rush production of 2,500 miles of stranded copper wire covered with gutta-percha, then wrapped in hempen yarn and wound around with 18 strands of iron wire. Unfortunately, failure to consult with each other caused the companies to fabricate the two sets of cable with an opposite lay, or twist, of the wires—a fact not discovered until production of the cable was completed in the breakneck time of six months. As a result, an elaborate splicing technique had to be developed to keep the wires from unwinding under tension. Since the mass of cable was too bulky to be accommodated by a single ship, half was loaded aboard the British man-of-war *Agamemnon* and half aboard the U. S. frigate *Niagara*. Between them, the ships were to pay out cable for the distance between

---

* Knighted for his work on the telegraph cable, Thomson became Lord Kelvin. His analysis of the cable laying process, updated and formulated into working rules, is still the standard mathematical treatise on the subject.

Valencia Island, off the coast of Ireland, and Trinity Bay, New-foundland.

In the year that followed, the crises and disasters that took place would have defeated a man of fainter heart than Field. On six different occasions the cable broke—once in 2,000 fathoms of water, whereupon more than 300 miles of line worth $500,000 were lost on the ocean floor. Repeatedly the line went dead, for intervals of minutes to hours, then mysteriously recovered. Storms of unprecedented fury battered the cable ships, which were further endangered by the shifting of their heavy cargoes in the holds. Twice, the ships were forced to abandon their mission and return to England for extra cable.

As might be expected, Field also had trouble with the directors of the Atlantic Telegraph Company, many of whom began to sense that the term "risk capital" had taken on new meaning when connected with Cyrus Field and his scheme. All of these problems were forgotten, however, when *Niagara* and *Agamemnon* finally landed their cable terminals and the first message flashed haltingly from Newfoundland to Ireland in August, 1858.

THE CANKER AT THE CORE

Wild jubilation on both sides of the Atlantic greeted the opening of the first transatlantic telegraph cable. Queen Victoria, in a 98-word message that took 16½ hours to transmit, congratulated President James Buchanan, who returned the compliment with a message that took 10 hours. Field was the hero of the day. But the cable itself was sick and dying of a thousand old wounds; signals were weak, messages became unintelligible, and, on October 20, 1858, it lapsed into silence altogether. An investment of $2.5 million lay at the bottom of the Atlantic. Field, now in disgrace, was accused of having rigged the fiasco for stock promotion purposes.

There were so many reasons for the failure of the cable that the real wonder is that it ever worked at all. Although the scientific theory underlying the submarine cable was as sound as Morse, Wheatstone, Thomson, and others had postulated, the practical part of the undertaking had been rushed into headlong, without anything approaching adequate preliminary preparation. Production of the cable had proceeded without proper standards and specifications. Part of the line had been left on a seaside wharf for months, exposed to hot sunlight which softened the gutta-percha and displaced the central wire. Some portions of it had been coiled and recoiled ten times over, rupturing the armor wires; some had been damaged in the holds of the storm-tossed ships. With egregious bad judgment, a company electrician had insisted on applying test potentials of 2,000 volts to the cable core—an altogether excessive amount that weakened the core and damaged its insulation.

The triumph of which Field was deprived in 1858 came to him eight years later, but not without another near-disaster. This time, the famous British ship, *Great Eastern*, was commissioned to carry out the cable laying operations. But in July, 1865, just as the *Great Eastern* had completed two-thirds of its journey across the Atlantic, the cable broke and 1,200 miles of line went to the bottom. However, a second voyage of the ship in July, 1866, was successful and, soon after, the broken cable was retrieved from the ocean floor, spliced with new cable, and safely landed at Newfoundland. Two working cables then linked the old and new worlds.*

THE MORE CAUTIOUS LEAP

It would be hard to imagine a contrast greater than that between the stormy saga of the first telegraph cable and the austere progression of its telephone counterpart. Where the telegraph had been rushed into transatlantic service while still in its

---

* The 1865 cable failed in 1877; the 1866 cable broke down in 1872 and was largely replaced in 1880. Many additional cables followed, and today there are more than 20 telegraph cables, largely unused, under the Atlantic.

Courtesy of Bell Telephone Laboratories, Incorporated

Great Eastern

technical infancy, the telephone was to grow into full maturity before taking the transoceanic leap in 1956.

There were several reasons for this. First of all, the transmission of speech currents is technically more demanding than the simple making and breaking of telegraph circuits. Even to obtain satisfactory speech transmission without distortion and noise over *land* lines was a formidable problem, requiring years of step-by-step improvement in technique. Secondly, the three developments that were to make transatlantic telephone feasible, the vacuum tube, carrier frequency transmission, and the coaxial cable, were all products of the twentieth century.

But there was another, more compelling reason as well: the cost of engineering failure had grown so great that investors had become far more cautious. The requirements of two great wars and of the world's most highly industrialized economy had

forced a more comprehensive approach. Gone for good were
the nineteenth-century inventor working in his garret and the
individual promoters, like Field, who viewed risks as chal-
lenges. In their stead was an all-out "crash program" technology
—involving the expenditure of vast sums of public or private
funds and the mobilization of great numbers of trained specialists.
At the same time, paradoxically, the chance of failure of a huge
technological enterprise—although greatly reduced by twentieth-
century scientific methods—not only was *not eliminated,* but
the cost of such failure increased directly in proportion to the
financial and human resources involved. In the case of the submarine telephone cable, this high cost of failure was to serve as a
powerful deterrent to any premature move to span the Atlantic.

LEARNING LESSONS ON LAND
Although barely a decade had elapsed between the opening of
the 1866 telegraph cable and Bell's invention of the basic mechanism of the telephone, only the most visionary—or farsighted—
at that time expected more than short-distance transmission
from the telephone. In essence, Bell had found that sound waves
set up in the air by the human voice would produce vibrations in
a thin metal diaphragm in a transmitter. If a magnet with an
electric current running through it were placed next to this diaphragm, it would turn the vibrations into variations in the
strength of the current. This fluctuating current, carried over a
wire to another electromagnet in a receiver, would produce vibrations in a metal diaphragm placed alongside it. These vibrations would duplicate the sound waves originally set in motion
at the transmitter and they would be heard by the listening ear
as a human voice.

Early telephone instruments were so crude that the general
public was largely unmoved by telephony until 1877, when Bell
demonstrated that his device would work over the distance from
Boston to New York. Then, within a decade, the Bell Telephone

Company acquired over 34,000 subscribers for service, mostly in cities and towns. The first telephone lines were of iron or steel wire strung along poles, and as service grew, a veritable forest of telephone poles sprang up, darkening the skies over the cities. In New York, 90-foot poles were to be seen with 30 crossarms and 300 open wires running between them.

Besides being unsightly, these masses of overhead wires created so many problems of interference and maintenance that the Bell Company developed cables, containing multiple pairs of wires, insulated from each other, to replace the tangle of open wires. As early as 1890, a cable containing 50 pairs of wires was installed in Philadelphia and became the forerunner of modern telephone cables. (In the next fifty years, the use of smaller wires, better insulation, and cable cores of improved design permitted the enclosure of over 2,000 pairs of wire in a single cable.) To increase the efficiency of its cables by reducing loss of signal strength, Bell introduced the first practical "loaded" cable in 1910. Inductance coils, containing magnetic cores that increased the inductance of the circuit and reduced attenuation of the signal, were placed at intervals of 3,000 to 6,000 feet along the cable lines. These reduced the electrical losses to the point where cable circuits could be three or four times as long as before. By 1913, coil loading made it possible to provide service from Washington to New York to Boston by underground cable and from New York to Denver by overhead wire.

BREAKTHROUGH 1: THE AUDION

Nevertheless, communication by telephone over great distances remained essentially out of reach until 1906, when Lee De Forest invented the audion vacuum tube and thereby opened the way for the development not only of long distance telephony, but of radio, television, radar, computers, and all the complex equipment of the electronic age. For the audion tube made possible the repeated amplification of continuous electrical currents to the point where they could span any distance required.

Briefly, the audion tube consisted of three elements, a filament and a plate with a grid in between, enclosed in an evacuated glass envelope. When heated by a direct current, the filament gave off electrons which were attracted to the positively charged plate, setting up an electronic flow through the tube. However, the charge applied to the third element, the grid, was not direct, but alternating current, which changed from negative to positive many times a second. When the charge was negative, the grid repelled electrons issuing from the filament and when it was positive, it attracted them, thereby producing an amplified alternating current through the tube. By sending a weak telephone signal through a series of such tubes, it could be built up to workable levels.

Before the audion could be used for telephony, however, a good deal of further work was necessary. To prevent gas from accumulating inside the tube, the vacuum was improved to the point where the tube could be operated as a pure electron conduction flow device up to a plate potential of more than 80 volts. Construction of the tube elements was altered to increase their rigidity and resistance to vibration. Increased electron emission and filament life of more than 1,000 hours were achieved by improvement in the oxide-coating on the filament elements. Thus it was not until 1913 that the first vacuum tube telephone "repeater" was placed in service. Two years later, the first coast-to-coast telephone circuit, employing six repeaters, opened between New York and San Francisco. Distance—at least on land —had been overcome in telephony.

BREAKTHROUGH 2: THE CARRIER WAVE

As experimentation with the vacuum tube continued, more of its remarkable properties came to light. It was found that if a portion of the output from the tube were fed back to reinforce the current going into it, the built-up current would be further amplified by the tube to produce a still larger current. In addition, it was discovered that if the amplification were great enough, a point would be reached at which the circuit would cease simply to amplify current and would begin to "oscillate"—i.e., generate periodic high frequency electromagnetic waves. From this vital discovery, there stemmed many marvelous developments, including the technique of "multiplex" carrier telephone, which made possible the transmission of many conversations simultaneously over a single pair of wires without interference with each other.

Simply stated, here is how the technique worked. Already known was the fact that voice frequencies fall naturally in the spectrum between 200 cycles and 3,000 cycles a second—each individual conversation requiring that span or "band width" of 2,800 cycles for satisfactory transmission of upper and lower voice tones. By means of carrier telephony, these voice frequencies were simply moved up into the portion of the spectrum between 5,000 and 25,000 cycles per second, where there would be a much roomier band width of 20,000 cycles to accommodate not just one, but many conversations. This elevation of the voice frequencies was accomplished by using the oscillating vacuum tube to generate high frequency waves in the 5,000 to 25,000 cycle range and by then imposing on them the lower range voice frequencies, an effect known as modulation. The voice frequencies rode along on the "carrier" waves without interference with each other, since their carrier waves were of different frequencies. Thus, over a single pair of wires there could be transmitted both a regular conversation in the 200 to 3,000 cycle range, several different transposed conversations in the 5,000 to 25,000 cycle range, and even simultaneous conversations in opposite directions—all kept apart by the different carrier frequencies to which they were assigned.

At the receiving end of the multiplex wires, the process was reversed by demodulation, bringing the transposed voice frequencies back down to their natural range. To separate out the various conversations at the receiving point, George A. Campbell, an American Telephone & Telegraph engineer, developed a remarkable device, basic to carrier technique, known as an electric wave filter.

By 1918, carrier telephony had developed to the stage where a line between Baltimore and Pittsburgh boasted four conversations, stacked above the voice channel, on a single pair of open wires. In the late 1920's, the technique was extended to telephone cables, thanks to a further important development by Harold S. Black of the Bell System, of the negative feedback amplifier. This ingenious device was invented after it was found that many more vacuum tube repeaters were needed for amplification of the high carrier frequencies than for regular voice frequencies because of the enormously greater loss of signal strength with distance at the higher frequencies. As telephone cables began to span longer and longer distances, a great deal of amplification had to be provided. Therefore, even minor imperfections in the individual vacuum tube repeaters could accumulate to serious proportions over the entire length of the lines. To reduce distortion, Black simply fed back a portion of the output of the vacuum tube repeater to its input—a procedure which ordinarily would amplify the distortions if the fed-back portions were of the *same* polarity as the input. However, if the feedback were made *opposite* in polarity to the input, the distortions in the feedback signal would be nearly cancelled out during its subsequent trip through the amplifier. This technique made it possible to add vacuum tube repeaters in great numbers to a telephone cable without impairing its transmission qualities.

As the number of telephone circuits and repeaters which could be packed into a single cable increased, a veritable revolution took place in the economics of telephony. Quite obviously, the vast savings in wire and cable which carrier technique made possible meant less investment required for multiline long distance systems—a consideration that was to weigh heavily in the decision to span the Atlantic.

BREAKTHROUGH 3: THE COAXIAL

While the early carrier systems transmitted at frequencies up to around 25,000 cycles, subsequent systems employed frequency bands reaching as high in the spectrum as 142,000 cycles and providing as many as twelve, two-way telephone circuits on overhead wires. As higher and higher frequencies were employed to supply the band widths required for multiple conversations, a new problem arose. For electromagnetic radiations act more and more like *radio* waves at higher and higher frequencies. As their frequency is boosted, they increasingly tend to leave ordinary wires and spread outwards in all directions in space. In order to confine these waves and guide them to their destinations, it became necessary to create a new type of transmission medium. The answer was found by putting one wire inside another to form a pencil-width copper tube with a wire running through it but separated from the tube walls by insulation. Sharing a common axis, this arrangement was known as the "coaxial" and it confined the waves all within the tube. The coaxial efficiently transmitted frequencies running into millions of cycles and provided hundreds of telephone channels. Furthermore, several coaxials could be grouped together to form coaxial cables, boosting the potential traffic still higher. In 1936, the first such cable, installed between New York and Philadelphia, carried a total of 240 simultaneous conversations.

With the advent of the coaxial cable to supplement the vacuum tube repeater and carrier wave technique, the technology of telephony reached a stage of maturity where the transatlantic cable was technically within reach. But now a new question arose: was it economically justifiable? For, in the years between

1915 and 1935, while telephony was growing up, so was radio. As a matter of fact, the vacuum tube itself, the feed-back amplifier, and the high frequency oscillator—all were originally developed for radio and subsequently pressed into the service of telephony. Experience with long wave radio for military use in World War I had produced rapid progress in ship-to-shore, ship-to-ship, and plane-to-ground radio telephony. In 1920, commercial broadcasting began in the United States and, in the mid-1920's, the discovery that radio signals are reflected between the earth and the ionosphere at successive points around the globe provided the basis for transcontinental broadcasting. In 1927, the Bell System inaugurated the first radio telephone service between New York and London. Now, at last, it appeared, the human voice could span the oceans of the world—and at only a small fraction of the cost of laying submarine telephone cables. But it was not to prove so easy. In the first full year of operation of the radio telephone service, an average of only seven transatlantic calls a day were made—primarily because disturbances in the ionosphere frequently made conversations unintelligible. Sometimes the signal was blanked out altogether for days at a time.

GUARANTEE: TWENTY YEARS

By the early 1930's, the growing numbers of people who *continued* to make use of the radio telephone, despite its shortcomings, prompted the Bell Company to launch a long-range program of research and development in vacuum tube technology and in the design of telephone repeaters especially constructed for submarine cables, to provide not one, but multiple, telephone circuits for transatlantic service. Sturdy, long-life tubes and components capable of operating dependably without maintenance for many years were developed by Bell engineers and proved by prolonged testing. As a result, the Bell Company by 1942 had evolved a plan for a postwar transatlantic cable—one providing twelve telephone channels, with vacuum tube repeaters to be placed at 50-mile intervals across the ocean floor. The plan was of only academic interest at the time, but it was becoming clear that a repeatered cable would be laid one day, and telephone engineers on both sides of the Atlantic were working and planning for that day.

Step by judicious step, the transatlantic cable began to move toward realization, and early in 1952, formal conferences on the subject were opened between American Telephone & Telegraph Company and the British Post Office.* From the start, both parties agreed that if the huge investment involved were to be justified, the cable system should be designed and built in such a way that it would operate flawlessly on the bottom, without maintenance of any kind, for at least twenty years. Failure of components, or any other contingency that might involve raising the cable, would interrupt service, causing loss of revenue and repair costs that might reach hundreds of thousands of dollars. Here, with a vengeance, was to be a challenge to the "tooth of time."

To the initial discussions, each country's representatives brought different ideas—based on their differing experiences—as to how to proceed. The British, who led the world in the total mileage of submarine cable produced and put down, were expert in the field of shallow water cables such as those linking the British Isles with the Continent. In 1943, they had installed the first submerged vacuum tube repeater in a telephone cable between Wales and the Isle of Man, and had followed this in 1947 with a coaxial cable providing the unheard-of total of 84 telephone channels between England and Holland. Even as the discussions with the Americans began, they were completing the design of a 36-circuit cable with seven repeaters for a deep-sea link between Scotland and Norway. This design, which the British privately anticipated would serve as the model for a trans-

* In England, communications are government-owned.

atlantic cable, embodied several of the most up-to-date concepts in submarine telephony: two-way transmission over a single cable; vacuum tube repeaters containing two separate sets of parallel amplifiers to provide continued operation in case either set failed; and late model electron tubes, with a high degree of amplification, to handle the high carrier wave frequencies needed to accommodate a large number of telephone circuits.

The British design had one important limitation, however. The repeaters consisted of rigid steel cases, 9 feet long by 10 inches in diameter—large enough to house the many components needed for two-way transmission and parallel amplification, but requiring special laying techniques. In order to ease each of these heavy units into the sea, it was necessary to stop the cable ship while lengths of the cable, weighing many tons, hung under tension between ship deck and ocean bottom—a situation of no great moment in shallow water, but dangerous in deep seas where the changing strain on the heavy suspended cable could cause unwinding and twisting of the spiral wires that served as the cable's outside armor.

The Americans, with a far less formidable array of installations to their credit, had greater expertise in deep-sea cables than the British, and had acquired considerable knowledge as a result of their work, going back to the 1930's, in vacuum tube repeaters designed specifically to withstand pressures as great as 6,800 pounds per square inch in waters 13,000 to 14,000 feet deep. These repeaters consisted of 17 sections, each no more than 6 inches long and less than 3 inches in diameter. Each section contained three vacuum tube amplifiers and 60 other components, flexibly joined together—somewhat like sausage links—in such a way that they could pass around the drum and sheaves of a cable ship and be payed out continuously as part of the cable itself, without the necessity of stopping the ship. The damaging effect due to twisting of the cable, with accompanying strain on the outside armor wires, was thereby eliminated.

Besides being easier to lay, the flexible repeaters contained vacuum tubes built to such conservative specifications that they could be depended upon to perform almost indefinitely, although with limited efficiency. The first American cables using "flexible" repeaters—two 100-mile lines, each with 24 channels and three repeaters—had been put down in 1950 between Key West and Havana and had proved maintenance-free and completely dependable. For this reason, the Americans fully expected that these cables would be the prototype for the transatlantic system.

However, in the American repeater design—as in the case of the British rigid repeater—there was a serious limitation. Its small size precluded the number and variety of components necessary to provide two-way transmission over a single cable. Signals could be transmitted one way only—necessitating the laying of *two* cables to provide service in both directions.

REACHING A CONSENSUS

Not surprisingly, both the British and the Americans tended to favor the type of repeater with which they were more familiar. To the British, the American proposal that flexible repeaters be used for the transatlantic link had somewhat the same incongruity of the Ford Motor Company's inviting the makers of the Rolls Royce to join forces to bring out a Model A. The vacuum tubes in the American repeater had been designed in the 1930's, the British pointed out, and were actually obsolete, providing only one-sixth the amplification of the tubes used in the rigid repeater. Moreover, this limited performance restricted the band widths and hence the number of cable channels to 36, compared with the 60 channels provided by the more sophisticated rigid repeater. Above all, a *pair* of cables would be more costly—and potentially twice as vulnerable to accident—as would a single rigid-repeatered cable.

To these objections, the Americans responded that their Key

West–Havana cables were existing proof that flexible repeaters performed dependably in deep seas, whereas there was no example extant of a rigid repeater operating in any but shallow waters. Furthermore, they added, since utmost reliability and long life were the criteria agreed upon for the cable, the rugged 1930-vintage pentode vacuum tube and other thoroughly tested components of the flexible repeaters were clear advantages rather than otherwise. Finally, the American repeaters could be laid continuously by a conventional cable ship without special equipment or techniques.

The reasoned manner in which final agreement was reached by the British and the Americans on the design of the cable might well serve to confound all nationalists. It had already been agreed that the undersea system was to consist of two sections—a link of 400-odd miles from Sydney Mines, Nova Scotia, to Clarenville, Newfoundland; and a link of about 2,500 miles from Clarenville to Oban, Scotland. Since the waters between Nova Scotia and Newfoundland were only about 250 fathoms, at the deepest, it was decided that the British system would prevail there. A single cable would be put down with 16 rigid repeaters, spaced at 25-mile intervals, to provide a total of 60 two-way voice channels in the portion of the frequency spectrum between 20 kc.-260 kc. for eastern, and 312 kc.-552 kc. for western transmission. Then in the ocean waters between Newfoundland and Scotland—as deep as 2¼ miles—the American system would be used, with two cables to be laid about 20 miles apart. Each would have 51 flexible repeaters, spaced every 40 miles, providing 36 voice channels of 4 kc. apiece in the portion of the spectrum between 20 kc.-164 kc.

Once this basic decision was reached, further details were soon worked out and, in November, 1953, contracts were signed by the participants in the project, American Telephone & Telegraph Co., the British Post Office, and Canadian Telecommunication Corp., to start construction of the cable and its associated components. Under the joint venture, the Americans were to manufacture the 102 flexible repeaters and a small amount of associated cable. The British were to provide the 16 rigid repeaters and 95 per cent of the cable for the total system.* In addition, a British cable ship, H.M.S. *Monarch,* was to carry out the entire laying operation.

IN PURSUIT OF INFALLIBILITY

If it would appear that an unconscionable amount of looking-before-leaping had taken place in reaching the decision to proceed with the cable, so much is little in comparison with what followed. In order to guarantee that not one failure in twenty years would occur in any of the 402 vacuum tubes and 10,800 other components in both the shallow and deep-sea sections of the cable, the most extraordinary production procedures and standards were adopted by both the Americans and the British. As one observer put it: "Submarine cable engineering is not just conservative—it's reactionary." At the plant in Hillside, New Jersey, converted by Western Electric Company, a manufacturing subsidiary of A. T. & T., to manufacture the flexible repeaters, employees dressed in special dust- and lint-proof clothing—working in conditions of almost hospital cleanliness—painstakingly fitted together the 900 parts making up the narrow repeaters. Specifications were so rigid that less than 10 per cent of the long-life electron tubes produced for the repeaters and tested for 5,000 hours were accepted for actual use. Rejections of other components, such as capacitors, inductors, and resistors routinely ran between 20 and 50 per cent. All in all, the repeaters underwent such meticulous assembly, testing, and historical documentation that a year was required to complete each —at an initial cost of $70,000 apiece.

---

* A tidy historical touch was supplied by the fact that the manufacturer of the cable was a subsidiary of the original firm that produced the 1866 telegraph cable.

To appreciate why this care was necessary, it is important to remember that the deep-sea repeaters were the very heart of the transatlantic cable. Even on land, it is necessary to have repeaters every twenty miles or so to overcome loss of signal strength. Consider, then, that in a submarine cable, loss at the high frequencies involved is so great that signals must be amplified by a factor of *a million every 40 miles* if they are to be usable. Thus, with 51 repeaters, each boosting the signal a million-fold, the total amplification made possible by the system was in the order of 10 raised to the power of 306—an awesome figure that could be reduced to zero instantly by the failure of a single tube or component. Moreover, the lack of accessibility of the repeaters for adjustment or replacement of parts; the high voltages required to power all of the repeaters in "series"; the chance of chemical deterioration of components due to interaction of gases contained in their materials; the enormous pressures at the bottom of the sea; the hazards of shock and vibration in laying—all these factors dictated that no effort be spared to insure the integrity of the deep-sea repeaters. Toward this end, nearly five hundred specialists in more than fifty separate departments of Bell Laboratories diligently applied themselves. Of this number, approximately 75 per cent were mechanical and electrical engineers, with mathematicians, physicists, and chemists making up the balance.

While the repeaters—both flexible and rigid—quite naturally received the most concentrated attention of any part of the system, the cable itself was by no means a routine manufacturing job. Produced under strict standards to prevent any irregularities that might affect transmission, it represented the largest-diameter cable ever laid in deep water—a factor aimed at helping to reduce signal loss. The 5,000-odd miles of deep-sea line, with an outside diameter of 1¼ inches, were composed of a central copper wire surrounded by nine layers of materials: helically wound copper tapes, polyethylene insulation, the coaxial copper return conductor, additional layers of copper, jute and cotton tape, armor wires, and an outer layer of impregnated jute. The 400-odd miles of shallow-water line, with an outside diameter of 2 inches, were provided with still more layers of insulation and armor wires to protect them from trawlers, currents, and other hazards. Once manufactured, the cable was carefully stored in tanks through which temperature-controlled water was constantly circulated—a far cry indeed from the battered coils of the first telegraph cable, lying in a heap on the deck under the sun.

THE TESTING

So it was that the day came, less than two years after the international cable agreement was signed, for the H.M.S. *Monarch* to proceed with laying the cable in the Atlantic. All was in readiness. Like pearls of great price—which indeed they were—the finished flexible repeaters had been flown, carefully supervised, to England and spliced into every 40 miles of cable. Crews had been rehearsed in the techniques of paying out cable and repeaters in both deep and shallow waters. Transmission tests of the line had been made and evaluated. Yet, ironically, as precautions against failure increased, so—in a sort of perverse ratio—did doubts of success. In the words of one Bell engineer: "I kept waking up at night thinking of all that money's going to the bottom of the ocean and wondering what we'd say to the stockholders if the thing didn't work." But this time, in contrast to the similar nineteenth-century enterprise, the prevailing attitude had been, "Plan the thing so carefully, and make it so perfectly that it can't possibly fail to work."

As a result, the actual laying of the telephone cable turned out to be such an uneventful, businesslike, methodical performance—and it attracted so little attention—that most people on both sides of the Atlantic were unaware of it. By contrast with the avid interest of mid-nineteenth-century Americans in all details of the first telegraph cable, the bland indifference that greeted the achievement of the telephone cable stands out with startling clarity.

Late in June, 1955, with no fanfare, the *Monarch* left Clarenville, Newfoundland, with its first consignment of cable and repeaters which it payed out in the relatively less deep waters to the drop-off of the Continental Shelf. Marking the end of the cable with a buoy, the ship sailed to England, where it took aboard 1,500 miles of deep-sea cable and repeaters, returned to the buoy, spliced the cable, and headed back at an average speed of 6½ knots to Scotland. At the Rockall Banks, the ship marked the end of the deep-sea cable with another buoy and proceeded to England to load 500 additional miles of armored cable. On returning in a storm and finding that the buoy had disappeared, the *Monarch* waited for calm, grappled for the cable, retrieved it, spliced it to the cable aboard, then completed the last lap to Oban, Scotland. By the end of September, 1955, the east-bound cable was complete and operating, and the following June, the *Monarch* repeated the entire process in reverse, completing the west-bound cable in mid-August, 1956.

Excluding time in transit and loading, only 40 days were needed to lay both east and west links of the cable. No line was lost on the bottom. No signal trouble occurred. From the day it went into operation, the cable worked perfectly. Within two weeks after service began, transatlantic traffic of about two thousand telephone conversations a week was reached. After three years of service, the cable—which represented an investment of $42 million—had become a dependable contributor to the dividends of one and a half million A. T. & T. stockholders. With more than half of its twenty years of guaranteed life behind it, the cable has shown no sign of deterioration, and there has been not a single component failure—although it has been broken several times by trawlers and repaired at a cost of approximately a quarter of a million dollars each time.

TAT-I TO TAT-III

The brilliant success of TAT-I—as the first transatlantic telephone cable came to be known—pioneered a whole decade of ocean telephone cables that totalled 27,130 nautical miles and soon reached around the world. In October, 1963, when the latest cable, known as TAT-III, first began operations, the volume of transatlantic telephone calls via submarine cable had grown from an average of three hundred per day in 1956 to about two thousand per day; by the end of 1965, the average volume had grown to seven thousand calls per day.

There appears to be no limit to the urge of people on both sides of the Atlantic to talk with each other on the telephone. What new technologies can help satisfy this vast urge in the future? In addition to the now-classical vacuum tube telephone cables, there is another—one based on the use of transistors—which provides many hundreds of voice channels over a single cable and has prospects of a life span several times that of earlier cables. Specially-equipped satellites, strategically located in the skies over the ocean, can and do serve as telephone repeaters—receiving, amplifying, and transmitting signals broadcast from microwave radio antennas on land.

In any case, whatever form transatlantic voice communication may eventually take, it is sure to rest securely for many years to come on the engineering integrity of the TAT cables and their remarkable defiance of the "tooth of time."

machina
ex
machina

"THE REVOLUTION STARTS THIS SUMMER," announced the editors of the *Harvard Business Review* in 1954. "The acquisition of the first Univac to be used in business may eventually be recorded by historians as the foundation of the second industrial revolution."

The occasion of this sweeping prediction was the delivery of a Remington Rand Universal Automatic Computer to General Electric Company's Appliance Park in Louisville, Kentucky. Although a few Univacs had been purchased by the United States Government in the early 1950's for use by the Census Bureau and other agencies, the decision by General Electric to install one of the machines to handle payrolls and billing, schedule materials, control inventory, and perform other routine accounting functions marked the first time that business had turned to an electronic computer to help harness the flood-tide of paper work generated by the nation's booming postwar economy.

THE SECOND INDUSTRIAL REVOLUTION

In the years that followed General Electric's first bold step, the revolution has taken place as predicted. But the speed with which it has occurred has been far beyond anything the *Harvard Business Review* could have foreseen. Today in the United States alone there are approximately 44,000 computers in use or on order, representing an investment of more than $12 billion. Their uses, which long ago outstripped the simple mechanization of clerical work, now extend from the control of automated industrial equipment and processes, to the solution of basic problems in advanced physics, the formulation of military strategy, the forecasting of the levels of national economic activity, and the diagnosis of disease. Some important developments—notably nuclear weapons, space probes, communications satellites, and early warning defense systems—would have been impossible without computers. Various types of the machines are used today to do everything from apprehending criminals, forecasting weather, tracing the paths of satellites and planets, making airline reservations, calculating the electric and magnetic fields of the atom, plotting the trajectories of missiles in flight, to designing ships and aircraft.

Computers have even been developed to program the building of more complex computers. Engineers working on the Nike-Zeus anti-ballistic missile defense system created conceptual diagrams for a key computer needed in the system, then fed information from the diagrams into another computer. The machine calculated detailed specifications for the new computer from circuit packages available, prepared a plan for placing the packages onto racks to go into equipment bays, made up parts lists and wiring specifications, and produced punched tapes to run the wiring machines that actually produced the Nike-Zeus computer. *Machina ex machina.*

Equally startling have been the developments on the industrial front. In Detroit, computer-controlled transfer machines turn out complete automobile engine blocks on an automated line as long as a football field, subjecting each one to five hundred separate processes. On the West Coast, aircraft companies employ computers to program contour milling machines capable of working any known metal into as many as 18 basic shapes *automatically*. In the Southwest, the oil industry has built catalytic cracking plants run by computers and a handful of technicians. Yet, at the same time, so many and varied are the skills involved in the designing, manufacturing, programming, and servicing of computers that, by 1970, computer-associated activities are expected to constitute the country's leading industrial occupation. In the meantime, the burgeoning computer market contributes heavily to the steady rise in the nation's gross national product.

By contrast with the cruel, uprooting dislocations of the first Industrial Revolution, the second seems to be proceeding in a benign, bloodless manner. No monstrous industrial wastelands have been spawned; no wrenching shift of power has taken place among classes; no deep cultural shock has been recorded so far. And although an occasional shiver of apprehension runs through the ranks of the humanists, recalling "Rossum's Universal Robots" in Karel Čapek's *R. U. R.,* and although Norbert Weiner and other scientists have been concerned, still there is no evidence of any widespread feeling that mindless automata are taking us over. On the contrary, it is as though the computer has been drawn to the center of the nation's economy to fill a huge vacuum of need, the true dimensions of which were not even suspected. We may still be just beginning to grasp them.

How has all of this come to pass? As late as 1950, computers were looked upon primarily as laboratory curiosities. Their critical use during World War II for military purposes—largely secret—had involved calculations so esoteric that even computer enthusiasts foresaw a future containing no more than a dozen or so of the machines for use in highly specialized scientific or government work. Then in the early 1950's, International Business Machines Corporation, the dominant company in the office machinery field, hesitantly undertook developmental work on a production-line computer for scientific calculations known as the 701 Defense Calculator. Unsure of the potential market for such a machine, the company sought at least 13 firm defense contracts (from companies manufacturing arms and supplies for the Korean War) before committing itself to production. When orders for 19 of the 701's were forthcoming, IBM entered the computer business in 1952.

What followed made industrial history in the United States. Although Remington Rand was the leader in computer design and in research and development of the computing art, IBM was in a position to back up its technical competence with a well-established sales engineering and marketing organization that had been built up during its years of dominance of the punch card–office machinery business. With this organization ready to promote, install, and service its machines and to educate customers in their use, IBM designed and built a total of 17 different types of computers in its famed "700-7000 Series" in the next decade, overtaking and surpassing every other company in the field. Engineered, programmed, and priced to fit the requirements of medium-sized as well as large users and to perform a great variety of functions, this versatile and widely popular family of computers proved to be the decisive factor in the computerization of United States industry.

EARLY ENGINES

The meteoric rise of the computer to its present eminence tends to overshadow the facts that the principles on which it is based are far from new and that its evolution has been marked by periods of dormancy as well as progress. The first of all mechanical calculators, the abacus, was invented independently by the Greeks and the Chinese some twenty-five centuries ago— it is still used by half the world today. The binary numbers system, on which modern computers are based, is thought to have originated with the Chinese around 2000 B.C. Seventeenth-century Europe made fundamental contributions to the art of calculation: John Napier invented logarithms and Henry Briggs worked out their tables; Edmund Gunter plotted logs on a ruler and William Oughtred invented the slide rule; Blaise Pascal, the French philosopher, built an adding machine with numbers geared to each other by a pin-wheel mechanism; Gottfried von Leibnitz, the German philosopher-mathematician, designed a machine using a stepped wheel which could multiply by fast addition, still the primary method used even in high-speed computers.

A full century elapsed before further significant progress was made. Then, in 1812, Charles Babbage, an English mathematician, while checking some intricate calculations for the British Astronomical Society, found so many errors that he remarked in exasperation to a colleague, "I wish to God these calculations had been made by steam!" To which the other replied, "It is quite possible." This was hardly a profound response, but it nevertheless set Babbage off on an obsessive, lifelong search for a machine capable of performing all types of mathematical computations.

Babbage's first attempt at the machine, known as his Difference Engine, used a logarithmic table to compute polynomial equations. Accurate to six decimal places, the machine was the first ever devised to provide for the simultaneous, or "parallel," carry-over of digits in mathematical computations. Not satisfied with this order of capability, Babbage designed another machine with accuracy to 20 decimal places. Then, finding himself frustrated by the lack of levers and cog wheels of proper precision,

Charles Babbage

he abandoned this idea and turned to the creation of a new machine, the Analytical Engine, which was to be at once his greatest achievement and cause of his bitterest disappointment.

BABBAGE'S GRAND DESIGN

In its fundamental concept and organization, the Analytical Engine was the first true computer and the logical forerunner of all subsequent generations of the genre. Although the basic arithmetic was nothing more than simple addition, Babbage had worked out a way to manipulate additions so as to produce subtractions by adding to a number the so-called "9's complement" of the number to be subtracted.* He obtained multiplications by adding a number to itself the required number of "times" and shifting, and divisions by successively adding to a dividend the 9's complement of its divisor until the point of zero or a decimal fraction was reached and shifting. He also devised a method of using punch cards, developed for rug looming by the French inventor Joseph Jacquard, to feed data into the engine and retrieve results from it. He designed a "store" section of the machine to be stocked with large quantities of numbers (Babbage envisioned a thousand of 50 digits each); a "mill" section, where all calculations would be carried out through the rotation of steam-powered gears and wheels; and an independent collection of gears and levers to fetch numbers from store to mill and then put them back. There was even an astonishingly advanced provision in the design which permitted the engine to transfer from one calculation to another, under certain conditions, without the intervention of any human agent. For instance, if the result of a given computation turned out to be a negative number, gears could be set to go into action, putting aside the computation and activating the selection of another problem to be solved.

In short, the plan of the Analytical Engine possessed many of the basic components of later generations of computers: input-output devices, "memory" or storage of data and program, a calculating unit, overall controls, and "conditional transfer" or branching capability. Moreover, Babbage understood very clearly that the basic role of the machine was to employ arithmetic of the most primitive kind to perform thousands of tedious, repetitive calculations and to do it all *fast*. Because of the first condi-

---

* For example, instead of subtracting 702 from 963 to get 261, the same result may be obtained by adding to 963 the complement of 702—298—and throwing away the final 1 carried to the left.

An early calculating device

tion, he insisted on coupling a high order of accuracy with speed. By carrying results to 10 or even 20 decimal places, he could overcome errors that build up when great numbers of sequential calculations are successively "rounded off." Once a vast volume of fast, highly accurate, elementary arithmetic became available, the operator of the machine could then use it to produce calculations of any degree of sophistication required.

Like Babbage himself, the concept of the Analytical Engine was far in advance of the times. Contemporary machine tools and metal working techniques were simply not up to the close tolerances and ingenious arrangements called for in Babbage's complex plans. Although a less elaborate machine could have been built, and doubtless would have been a commercial success, Babbage was constitutionally unable to settle for anything less than his grand design. An inarticulate man, with disillusioned eyes and a mouth like a steel clamp, he spent forty years and most of his personal fortune in a dogged, unsuccessful effort to build the Analytical Engine. Misunderstood by most of his associates—some of whom thought him quite mad—he found an unexpected ally in and an affinity with Lord Byron's daughter, Ada Augusta, Countess of Lovelace, who saw with great clarity what he was trying to do. Of the engine, she wrote, "It is capable under certain circumstances of feeling *about to discover* which of two or more possible contingencies has occurred and then shaping its future course accordingly." A more vivid description of conditional transfer would be hard to find.

After Babbage's death in 1871, a group of British scientists made a formal examination of the fantastic conglomeration of drawings, specifications, mechanical contrivances, and half-constructed parts that were the sum total of the Analytical Engine. They reached the epitaph-like conclusion that "the existence of an instrument of this kind would place within reach much which . . . had been too close to the limits of human endurance to be practically available." Babbage's work thereafter fell into obscurity, not to be rediscovered for seventy years.

BINARY AND BOOLE

It is uncertain whether Charles Babbage, amid his cranks and gears, knew of the work of a contemporary British mathematician named George Boole. If he did, it is doubtful that he saw a connection between that work and his own. Yet Boole's development in the 1850's of a new system of algebra based on symbolic logic and restricted to the two quantities, 0 and 1, laid the mathematical foundation for many future electric and electronic developments, including the logical design and engineering of computers.

As early as the seventeenth century, Leibnitz had rediscovered the ancient binary (base two) system, with its use of only two digits compared with the ten (0 to 9) of the decimal (or base ten) system. Simplest of all number systems, binary arithmetic builds entirely on progressive combinations of 0 and 1. Thus, the first binary digit is 0, the next is 1; but to represent 2, the binary system takes the next-largest number that can be made up from

0 and 1, namely 10. To get 3, the next-largest number is 11; 4 will be 100, and so on. So, the binary equivalents of decimal numbers between 0 and 9 are:

Decimal	Binary
0	0
1	1
2	10
3	11
4	100
5	101
6	110
7	111
8	1000
9	1001

Such a system made possible a form of arithmetic much less complicated than that of the ten-digit decimal system.* However, there was one obvious drawback to the binary system in the unwieldy length of the digits required to express even relatively small numbers. (For example, the binary equivalent of 50 is 110010.) Leibnitz concluded that this difficulty was so great as to make the system impracticable.

It remained for Boole, one hundred and eighty years later, to grasp the importance of the binary system to algebra and logic. In essence, he showed that there was a close analogy between algebraic symbols, the two binary values, and two-valued logic (true-false). Thus, if algebraic symbols, such as x, y, z, were used to stand for objects and properties of objects, such symbols might obey the same primary laws of combination as do numbers, making it possible to add, subtract, multiply, and

---

* In binary addition, two different digits added together produce 1, and two similar digits added together produce 0; and if both digits are 1, the machine must carry 1.

divide them.* Boole developed an algebra of propositions using binary digits connected with conjunctions such as *and/or* which could be treated like mathematical equations.

What neither Leibnitz nor Boole could have foreseen was that binary arithmetic would prove to be ideally suited to machine computation. The two unambiguous binary values, 0 and 1, lent themselves perfectly to electro-mechanical and electronic representation: a switch was either on or off; current flowed or did not flow; a number was positive or negative; an answer, yes or no. Moreover, calculating machines of the future were to operate at such fantastic speeds that the length of the numbers used became irrelevant. Finally, Boolean algebra set forth principles of logical organization that could be translated directly into the design of the two-state circuits of digital computers. And/or logic, implemented by switches, opened the way to the highly flexible operations of modern computers.

All of these developments, of course, lay far in the future. Although W. S. Jevons, the British economist, based a pure logic system on Boole's mathematical analyses and even constructed a syllogistic or "reasoning" machine in 1865 to show its accuracy, Boole's prophetic work soon followed that of Babbage into obscurity. By the time the curtain lifted again, World War II had begun.

THE COMPUTER RENAISSANCE

The modern age of the digital computer may be said to have dawned in the late 1930's at both Bell Telephone Laboratories and at Harvard University. At Bell Laboratories, Dr. George Stibitz drew on electro-mechanical relays and other components of telephone technology to design a machine capable of cal-

---

* Example: if x equals white and y equals horses, while the binary value 0 equals nothing and 1 equals everything, then the formulation $1 - x$ means all things except white things; and $(1 - x)(1 - y)$ means all things neither white nor horses.

culating with complex numbers (those having a real and an imaginary part). The complex calculator, as it was called, was the first machine to break away from the decimal system by coding decimal digits in such a way that they could be calculated internally by the binary system. Stibitz's machine was also the first used to demonstrate "computing at a distance." In order to supplement a lecture he was to give at a meeting of the American Mathematical Association at Dartmouth College in the fall of 1940, Dr. Stibitz arranged for a hook-up of teletypewriter circuits. These transmitted mathematical problems from Hanover, New Hampshire, to the computer in New York and returned the answers from New York to Hanover, where they were typed out automatically—a feat which dazzled his audience.

Meantime, at Harvard, Howard Aiken, a mathematics teacher and a candidate for a doctoral degree in physics, began experimenting with various adding and tabulating machines then on the market to help solve some intricate equations with which he was working. After devising several techniques to adapt the machines to the task at hand, he decided that a more promising approach would be to start from scratch and design one general-purpose machine capable of performing all types of mathematical calculations. When his work showed sufficient promise, he requested—and received—the backing of International Business Machines Corporation, which had a natural interest in furthering the cause of calculating machine design. Work on the Automatic Sequence Controlled Calculator, as it was known, began at IBM in 1939; five years later the finished machine was installed at Harvard, where it proceeded to revolutionize the calculation of mathematical tables.

The ASCC (also known as the Mark I) was the world's first fully automatic general-purpose computer and a natural child of Babbage's Analytical Engine, although Aiken was completely unaware of Babbage's work at that time. As in the case of that venerable contraption, data were placed in the machine by punch cards and stored in registers for future use. Computations took place in a central arithmetic area. Precise instructions expressed in numbers were punched onto a paper tape and fed into the machine in simple sequences—one instruction for each calculation. The large (51 feet by 8 feet) assembly was powered by electricity, and its basic operations were performed by the action of some 3,000 electro-mechanical telephone relays, as in the case of Stibitz's complex calculator. These consisted of metal bars which could be raised by the application of electromagnetic force and lowered by removing it, thereby breaking an electrical circuit or establishing it. With this equipment, ASCC performed a multiplication of two ten-digit decimal-system numbers in about 3 seconds. Regardless of how sophisticated the problem involved, of course, the machine accomplished its work by means of fast, simple addition—like a child counting on his fingers—recalling Alfred North Whitehead's comment that the great virtue of numbers is that they can be used to carry on long trains of reasoning without bothering about the subject matter.

The electro-mechanical computers were far more than experimental machines. The ASCC was scarcely completed when it received its first major assignment. Intelligence reports had indicated that the Germans were developing an electrically-powered cannon. To keep pace, the United States would be forced to channel talent and resources into a like effort; but first, it was decided to try to gauge the feasibility of the German scheme. After intensive computations and analysis of mathematical equations, the ASCC came up with the welcome answer: the cannon wouldn't work. The United States was free to concentrate on other projects—among them the atomic bomb.

THE MOORE SCHOOL GROUP

Even as Aiken and IBM were rushing the ASCC toward completion, two men at the University of Pennsylvania's Moore School of Electrical Engineering were at work on a very different computer development, called forth by the wartime emergency. In 1943, Dr. J. Presper Eckert, an electrical engineering teacher at the Moore School, and John Mauchley, a graduate student specializing in physics, had come up with a plan for a high-speed computer using *vacuum tubes* to replace the slower electro-mechanical relays. The need for such a machine had become pressing as a result of a joint project, conducted by the Moore School and the Aberdeen Proving Ground, to prepare artillery firing tables for use by the Army. Computations made by conventional means—primarily row upon row of girls using desk calculators—took so long that increased speed had become an urgent necessity.

The solution to the problem, provided by Eckert and Mauchley, was the Eniac (Electronic Numerical Integrator and Calculator), the first *electronic* computer. Completed in 1946, Eniac produced a multiplication in the unheard-of time of less than three-thousandths of a second, employed 18,000 vacuum tubes, used punch cards for input and output of data, and was "programmed" through the special hand wiring of its internal circuitry. Somewhat like a dishwashing machine, the cycle of operations was set in advance; to change the order of its operations meant re-wiring the circuits, a tedious, time-consuming job that took the better part of a day. Although Eniac was admirably suited to the repetitive work required for Aberdeen, its lack of flexibility limited its use in other, more diverse calculations.

Challenged by this programming difficulty, the Moore School group, even while working to complete Eniac, was thinking ahead to a new machine. By this time, in addition to Eckert and Mauchley, the talent available to the group included Dr. John von Neumann, a mathematician, logician, physicist, and consultant to both Aberdeen Proving Ground and the Los Alamos Atomic Laboratory; Lieutenant Herman Goldstine, an Army liaison officer and former professor of mathematics at the University of Michigan; and Dr. Arthur Burks, a member of Michigan's Philosophy Department. Joining their very considerable forces, the group began work on an electronic computer in which the plugged-in program would be replaced by a more flexible one. This was accomplished by building certain operations, such as "add," "multiply," "store," into the circuitry of the machine and assigning them numbers so that each operation could be called into play by its number. A sequence of these numbers, specifying the programmed sequence of operations, could be stored in the machine, along with the data to be processed, and activated to carry out the calculation. To change the program required changing only the stored numbers; no wiring change was necessary. This new method was known as stored program computing.* The result was the Edvac (Electronic Discrete Variable Automatic Computer), a machine which proved to be a basic mutation in the evolution of computing machines.

The implications of the stored program concept were enormous. By using certain "words" in his instructions, the programmer was able to specify and call into play both the data to be processed and the operations to be performed on them. Here was something new under the sun—but not by any means the only new feature of Edvac. The machine was the first electronic computer to employ the binary system of numbers and the first machine since the Analytical Engine to provide for conditional transfer. Under certain specific conditions—an answer of zero, for example—the machine was able to take an instruction out of sequence and move on to an entirely different set of calculations.

Completed and installed at Aberdeen Proving Ground in

* The stored program, along with other advanced concepts in computer design, was first described in 1946 in a series of papers by Burks, Goldstine, and von Neumann titled "Preliminary Discussion of the Logical Design of an Electronic Computing Instrument"—historic documents in computer annals. They were written at the Institute for Advanced Study for the Ballistics Research Laboratory.

1950, Edvac was the forerunner of a whole series of computers of major importance. The Edsac (Electronic Delay Storage Automatic Calculator), an almost identical machine, was built at the University of Cambridge and went into operation slightly before Edvac itself. The first and famed Univac, built by Eckert and Mauchley after they left the Moore School and set up in private business (soon acquired by Remington Rand), was delivered to the Census Bureau in 1951. Besides being the first commercially available computer with a stored program, Univac broke new ground by using metallic magnetic tape to put data into the machine and get it out—a method many times faster than punch cards. Although there were advantages in high speed for users such as the Census Bureau, with vast quantities of data to be handled, the actual calculating time of the Univac (a multiplication took about two-thousandths of a second) was relatively slow because of the repetitive, serial-type of computation involved.

In the meantime, IBM announced its SSEC (Selective Sequence Electronic Computer), the company's first large electronic computer. Combining 12,500 vacuum tubes with 21,400 electro-mechanical relays, the huge SSEC was designed specifically for scientific computations. It achieved fame as the computer used by investigators at Columbia University's Watson Scientific Computing Laboratory to trace the paths of Jupiter, Saturn, Uranus, Neptune, and Pluto back to the year 1653 and forward to the year 2060—a classic example of the type of mathematical drudgery that could have been borne only by a computer.

VON NEUMANN'S MACHINE

It was John von Neumann himself, however, who designed the most important successor to Edvac—perhaps the most important computer yet built. Returning to the Institute for Advanced Study at Princeton in 1946, in collaboration with Burks and

Goldstine, he set about to design an experimental machine which would go beyond stored programming to include various other revolutionary concepts of logical organization which he had been pondering for several years. The I.A.S. machine, as it was known, evolved slowly—it was not completed until 1952—but it succeeded in achieving a degree of operational sophistication that was to set the pattern for all subsequent computers.

What von Neumann did, in effect, was to carry much further the idea of storing instructions in the machine's memory. He showed the degree to which these instructions could be modified by the machine as it went along, changing the entire course of a computation, including the choice of data to be processed, without any human intervention whatever. This sophisticated "instruction modification," augmented by the relatively simple concept of conditional transfer, provided a highly advanced programming technique. The machine could be programmed to use the same group of instructions many times, transferring to a new set only after running through the group a prescribed number of times. Depending on the answer, it could then select one of two or more further groups of instructions to follow, calling up one or another of two or more different sets of data to be processed.

This ability of the I.A.S. machine to run through a series of such forked decisions, comparing, evaluating, and choosing its future course, in response to a relatively short program, opened up vistas even beyond those envisioned by Charles Babbage. In the words of one authority:

> . . . the amazing feature of a solution arrived at in this way, after thousands of operations based upon intermediate results and hundreds of decisions whose outcomes were unforeseen by the programmer, is that the final solution is so far removed from the data as to be much beyond our own mental powers. Suppose an engineering project requires the value of the maximum of some volume integral with two variable parameters, or an integral of a differential equation of the first order, or a manufacturing firm needs to know the composition or "mix" of ten kinds of goods

that will maximize profit. The answers to such perfectly routine problems are so much beyond our human powers unaided by the machine that to call them "unknown" is to use the same word with two different meanings. This puts the intellectual achievements of the machine as far above our own as the output of a large bulldozer is above that of a common laborer. In both cases, we have built a machine which accomplishes for us a task beyond our power.*

Besides developing the concept of instruction modification, the I.A.S. machine was the first to offer access at random to all the data stored in its memory, either for instant use or for updating. In Edvac and Univac, data had been stored in devices known as mercury delay lines, each of which held several hundred binary 0's and 1's, known as "bits," of individual information. To locate any single bit in such a memory, it was necessary for the machine to search the lines sequentially from end to end, a procedure that took several thousandths of a second. In another type of memory device in use, the magnetic drum, the bits were represented by magnetized spots on the surface of a revolving cylinder. To turn up a specified bit, the drum had to pass on the average through half of a revolution, requiring approximately the same length of time.

To reduce access time by eliminating the process of sequential searching, von Neumann and his colleagues turned to a type of cathode ray tube, developed by the British during the war for use in radar, to serve as the memory for this machine. By means of a technique known as electrostatic storage, binary digits representing bits of data were stored on the face of the tube in a pattern of negative-positive charge distribution. Forty of these tubes constituted the memory of the I.A.S. machine and provided access at random to any given bit in something like ten-millionths of a second. Although subsequent developments were

* Professor Philippe LeCorbellier, of the Harvard University Division of Engineering and Applied Physics, at a Harvard Symposium on Digital Computers and Their Applications, April, 1961.

to supplant electrostatic storage and provide even faster access to data, von Neumann's machine helped to break the bonds of sequential access.

The I.A.S. machine was widely copied throughout the United States and abroad, becoming the prototype for such distinguished machines as the Los Alamos Atomic Laboratory's Maniac (the Mathematical Analyzer, Numerical Integrator and Computer), which made computer history when its intricate calculations enabled the United States to build and test the hydrogen bomb ahead of the Soviet Union.* A later machine—IBM's 701 Defense Calculator—was to play a historic role of another kind, as we shall see.

M.I.T. AND MAGNETIC CORE MEMORY

The burst of creativity that took place in computer engineering between the start of World War II and the early 1950's, exemplified by the pioneering Mark I, Eniac, Edvac, and I.A.S. machines, reached a peak with the introduction of magnetic cores for computer memories. The cores were first installed in the early 1950's at the Digital Computer Laboratory of the Massachusetts Institute of Technology on Whirlwind I, a high-speed computer, built in the late 1940's by M.I.T. for the Navy and the Air Force.

The Laboratory staff, under the direction of Dr. Jay Forrester, was searching for a way to improve on the Whirlwind's original memory of two banks of 16 electrostatic tubes each of which provided 2,048 words of memory. Observing the behavior of particles of ferrite, iron oxide compounded with small quantities of nickel, copper, manganese, magnesium, etc., they conceived the idea of using magnetic cores. They had found that the internal magnetic field of such ferrites, when exposed to an external

---

* Other machines based on the I.A.S. are: Argonne National Laboratory's Avidac, Oak Ridge's Oracle, Aberdeen Proving Ground's Ordvac, the University of Illinois' Illiac, the University of Sydney's Silliac, and M.I.T.'s Whirlwind I.

magnetic field of sufficient strength, aligned itself with this external field and retained the alignment even when the external field was removed. If the external field direction was reversed, and had sufficient strength, the internal field of the ferrite would reverse itself and retain this new direction just as tenaciously.

Forrester's group decided that this characteristic of ferrite was ideally suited to the two-value binary system of modern computers. The M.I.T. group developed tiny rings or cores of compressed ferrite powder, with diameters of a few-hundredths of an inch, each capable of storing a binary digit. These cores were strung on wires, tennis-racquet fashion, so that each core had two sets of wires running through it at right angles to each other as well as a "sensing" wire which threaded all the cores in the plane. Equating the 0 and 1 digits of binary numbers with the two directions of the internal magnetic field of the ferrites, bits were "written in" to the magnetic cores by passing negative or positive pulses of electricity through one of the sets of wires in their centers. To "read out" what was in the cores, reverse current pulses were sent through the other set of wires in their centers. When the reverse pulses caused the cores to switch their directions, signals would be transmitted from the cores to the calculating unit of the machine. Thus individual cores could be "interrogated" and their contents read out: if there were a signal from a core, it would indicate that the core had previously been of the opposite direction; if no signal were transmitted, it would mean that the core did not switch and the polarity was unchanged. Selection of individual cores to be interrogated was accomplished by passing half-strength currents through certain perpendicular wires stringing the cores together. Only in the core where the two wires intersected would the full strength current occur, causing the core either to switch and transmit a signal, or remain unchanged.

Magnetic core memory solved at once a whole host of problems that had plagued computer engineers. The earlier delay line and vacuum tube memories were bulky, heat generating—necessitating air-conditioning equipment—and often undependable in operation. By contrast, hundreds of thousands of magnetic cores, which operated cold, could be packed side by side in "planes" like cells in a honeycomb to provide compact, nearly indestructible memories, capable of delivering access to any stored bit in a few-millionths of a second. In the case of Whirlwind I, for example, Forrester and his group were able to double the capacity of the machine's memory by installing 73,728 cores in less space than had been occupied by its former electrostatic memory.

OUT OF THE LABORATORY—FULL BLAST

Up until 1951, the world of the digital computer had been largely confined to research laboratories peopled by mathematical geniuses, logicians, engineers, physicists, and doctors of philosophy. Although the basic logical design of the machines had been fully achieved by Eckert, Mauchley, von Neumann, Forrester, and others, and although all of the components needed to build them were readily available, yet with the single exception of the Univac used by the Census Bureau no computer had ever been built for *sale* to a commercial customer. Then, suddenly, the lid came off. IBM discovered that there were eager takers for its 701 before the machine was even in production. Remington Rand succeeded in selling General Electric a Univac.* The great computer race was on.

The IBM 701 Defense Calculator, a lineal descendant of von Neumann's I.A.S. machine, was announced in 1952 as the first production-line electronic computer specifically designed to solve *scientific* problems. Since these generally involved rela-

* In addition to offering the first commercial electronic computer, Remington Rand produced both the first commercial computer with magnetic core memory and the first commercial transistorized computer, and it pioneered in the use of advanced forms of magnetic film for machine memory.

tively small input and output of data but lots of calculations, the machine at first used comparatively slow punch-card input-output, but its parallel-type arithmetic was five to twelve times faster than the two-thousandths of a second rate of the serial Univac, its electrostatic storage memory was twice the size of Univac's delay line memory, and random access to the 701's memory was up to 20 times faster than the sequential access of Univac.

When Univac nevertheless continued to enjoy a competitive advantage because of its fast tape action, IBM brought out the 702, the first business machine with magnetic *plastic* tape and punch cards, too. Although there were problems with plastic tape at first, such as easy breakage and the tendency of the magnetic iron oxide coating to form particles that caused errors, IBM engineers soon developed a coating with better adhesive properties and faster tape drive, capable of moving data into the computer at the rate of 15,000 bits a second. They also introduced vacuum columns to regulate the tape as it moved into the machine, taking up the slack and eliminating breaks.

The 702 represented a great step forward in practical "nuts and bolts" computer engineering.* IBM engineers worked out a system, used on all subsequent machines in the 700 series, to create the computers from individual building blocks or "modules," each with 8 vacuum tubes and their associated components and circuits, which could be plugged into a central connecting system and the whole encased in a plastic housing. Since the rectangular 12- by 6-inch modules were removable, repairable, and re-pluggable, they vastly simplified production and cut the cost of maintenance of the machines in the field. When trouble occurred on an installation, IBM servicemen simply unplugged the faulty module and replaced it with another identical one,

---

* Paralleling the development of the 702 was that of the popular 650, an intermediate-size electronic computer handling both business and scientific computations, that became known as the workhorse of the industry.

often making the necessary repairs right at the customer's plant. In some instances the modularity principle also permitted the upgrading of the machines to higher levels of capability by adjusting the number of modules—or even whole sections of the machine containing several hundreds of modules—accordingly.

Both the 701 and 702 soon established their usefulness by such feats as the performance, in about an hour, of the 8 million calculations needed to solve a differential equation in aircraft wing design—work that would have taken a man using a desk calculator approximately seven years.* Encouraged by its experience with the machines, IBM joined forces with M.I.T.'s Lincoln Laboratory to develop for the Air Force a huge computer combining features of both the 701 and the Whirlwind for use in an early warning radar system. Known as SAGE (Semi-Automatic Ground Equipment), the system was the first ever devised to interpret "real-time" (as it happens) data gathered by United States radar networks and to assign protective defensive forces. Continuous information from outlying radar stations was fed over telephone lines to a command control center where it could be instantly analyzed and translated into visual displays, permitting decisions for action within a few seconds after its being received. The most taxing assignment ever undertaken by computer engineers up until that time, SAGE involved IBM in advanced reaches of computer technology and reinforced the company's decision to enter full-scale commercial computer production.

FASTER, STILL FASTER

In the decade following the introduction of the 701, IBM set the industry pace for the design of new, large, fast computers with increasingly greater capabilities. Continuing its policy of

---

* A descendant of the 702, the IBM 1401, was to become the most popular computer ever built. Developed as a low-cost system for smaller users, the 1401 is said to have accounted at one time for one-third of all the computers in use in the United States.

tailoring machines to fit the needs of customers, IBM in 1954 brought out the 704 and the 705, faster and more powerful versions of the 701 and 702 machines. The 704 had a magnetic core memory of 4,096 words (eventually 32,768 words)— twice that of the 701—and possessed such improvements as memory indexing (which greatly simplified repetitious calculations by reducing the number of instructions required) and floating point arithmetic (which permitted more efficient use of space in the arithmetic unit and reduced programming complexity).

By the middle of the decade, as more and more companies joined in the rush to computers to solve their data processing problems, a sort of shock wave began to sweep through the ranks of corporate personnel who found themselves confronted by the shiny new machines. Who was to operate the computers once the installation teams packed up and left? Top management, too, was unsettled by the need to engage in a form of self-analysis to determine how the machines could be most productively used. As one industrialist wryly observed, the really smart way to make use of a computer was to order it for delivery in eighteen months, reorganize the entire business to get ready for it, and then cancel the order. Intended to solve problems, the computers, at least initially, appeared to raise some instead.

Aware of the near-traumatic impact of the machines on their users, IBM launched an intensive effort to develop a simplified computer programming system that could be used by its customers' regular personnel to write programs for the machine. Although some basic work in algebraic formula translation had been carried out at M.I.T. and in Germany, much remained to be done in developing a complete, workable programming language. The result was FORTRAN (Formula Translator), introduced by IBM in 1956 to stimulate sales of its new 704 machines.

BREAKING THE LANGUAGE BARRIER

Ever since Babbage, the job of *instructing* calculating machines to carry out the tasks assigned to them had been viewed as an unfortunate, unavoidable drawback to the art of mechanical computation. The first digital computers required so much human attention at each stage—the selection of problems that could be effectively handled by the machines in the first place, the statement of the problems in terms of the logic of the machines' circuitry, and the step-by-step sequence of the program—that the productive use of the machines lagged well behind their rapidly developing technology. When the binary system of numbers came into general use for computers, the problem of communicating with the machines in this new foreign tongue became even more pressing.

The first attempt to bridge the gap between human language and the moronic 0's and 1's of the computers was the development by programmers of a system using the letters of the alphabet and decimal numbers in their instructions. They assigned binary code numbers to each of the 26 letters and to each of the decimal numbers from 0 to 9, and then stored these codes in the machine's memory. The programmers could then use convenient phrases for their instructions as CLA (Clear and Add), TRA (Transfer Control), DIV (Divide), which could be translated by the machine into its native 0's and 1's. In each problem, of course, the programmer had to provide specific one-for-one instructions for every step to be taken, supply addresses in the memory where the data were to be found, specify the operations to be performed and the locations where results were to be stored, etc. If any step should be omitted or any erroneous detail provided, the result would be chaos. Even with the aid of convenient phrases, programming required expertise and precision.

The introduction of FORTRAN reduced these requirements and helped launch the IBM 704 by reducing the language barrier between man and machine. In two years of concentrated effort, the IBM task force created a packaged computer-language program to translate a programmer's specifications, written in a sort of pidgin mathematical English known as FORTRAN language, into instructions for the machine.

The packaged program took the form of a complete set of punched cards ready to serve as input to the machine for storage in the computer's memory. There it provided the translation function described above, plus a sort of library of standard FORTRAN procedures, including an error-monitoring capability, for future reference. With the computer thus equipped in advance, the programming role of the client company's operative was reduced to specifying in FORTRAN language the data and the appropriate routines. In reducing the drudgery of programming, the FORTRAN group made one of the most important contributions in the history of computer technology.

SELLING A SERVICE

With the introduction of FORTRAN, IBM moved ahead determinedly to sell not just a machine, but an entire service, including installation, programming, and maintenance. To reinforce the effort, the company called on its Applied Science Group, 425 carefully selected technicians, many of whom held advanced degrees in mathematics, physics, and engineering, whose specific job it was to show prospective customers how an IBM computer could be used to solve their problems. An Applied Science representative, eager to help sell an IBM computer to a manufacturer of automobile generators, for example, would first immerse himself in the design problems involved in building a generator. Starting with something like a hundred pieces of basic individual data (the number of windings on each coil, the diameter and length of the wires, the resistance, etc.) he would

figure out how to use the computer to calculate what a generator with these physical parts would produce in terms of heat,
volts, and amperes of output and how much equipment it would
drive.

Since such a problem involved approximately a million calculations and would take an engineer using a desk calculator
a full year to solve, IBM's Applied Science representative
would obviously have a most persuasive sales argument if he
could show that the computer could handle the problem in a
few minutes. Equally important, he could show that such fast
action opened up unlimited vistas to the generator designer,
making it possible for him to try any number of variations of the
basic specifications in order to arrive at an optimum design in
terms of size, power, cost, or any other criterion he might select.
Without a computer, the investment in time necessary to perform
the computation involved would have made such experimentation prohibitively costly.

The success of the Applied Science Group with the 704 was
reflected in the fact that by mid-1956, IBM had delivered 76
of the machines and had booked orders for another 193. Used
extensively to design and track guided missiles, to monitor missile trajectories, and to solve problems in turbine blade design
and particle accelerator design, the 704 was, moreover, the first
computer employed to design another computer: engineers working on Pilot, a computer under construction for the National
Bureau of Standards, used a 704 both to figure out the circuitry
for the machine and to set up a maintenance program to diag-
nose any future difficulty in its operation. The 704 also made its
mark as the first computer to translate English into Braille.

The business counterpart of the 704, the 705, was promoted
with equal virtuosity by IBM. In one instance, which revealed
with great clarity how to combine technical skill with sales engineering, the company studied specifications released by the
United States Government for a computer to handle a huge pay-

check system, and moved quickly to work out a program to process the enormous input data by means of its 705 machine. Although the specifications had been painstakingly worked out for the Government by another company, which had high hopes of landing the order, the Government chose the IBM computer, because it had behind it the services of the Applied Science Group as well as the large, well-trained IBM maintenance staff.

With the launching of the 704 and the 705, IBM began to move ahead in the computer race and during 1956 the company decisively overtook Sperry Rand's Univacs.* At the same time, however, more companies began to enter the competition: Burroughs, Control Data Corporation, Philco, and others. To strengthen its lead, IBM in 1957 announced the 709, a sophisticated version of the 704, with a 32,768-word memory; simultaneous write-in, read-out, and computing ability, made possible by a data synchronization unit; and an increase in the data input rate to 62,500 magnetic tape bits per second.

To many it now seemed that the time had come to ask: what was the advantage of all this speed? Computers performing millions of calculations per second had now become standard, and still the drive for faster machines continued unabated. The answer was, as Babbage knew so long ago, that speed was mandatory in order to carry out the gargantuan quantities of "cheap" arithmetic which computers used to achieve their complicated results. In the case of a guided missile with a built-in computer, the path of the missile had to be capable of alteration during flight. Knowing the position and velocity of the missile in the air, the computer would have to calculate the current trajectory and estimate whether it would pass through the target. If not, circuits would have to be activated to change the course of the missile accordingly.

With increased computer speed, of course, came increased

* Remington Rand had merged with the Sperry Corporation in 1955.

need for reliability. Machines performing tens of thousands of calculations a second could not be permitted a fault rate of even one error in a hundred million operations, since this would result in the unacceptable risk of a mistake every minute and a half. To enhance the reliability of its machines, IBM introduced new methods of programming, systems design, quality control, and the precision tooling of both computer components and electro-mechanical parts such as tape units and disk files.

The speed and reliability of the 709 proved to be so great that it soon became the workhorse machine for complex scientific assignments of all kinds. These included its use in Project Mercury to process and send back from the Bermuda tracking station to the Goddard Space Flight Center real-time data on the location and position of space capsules.

TRANSISTORS TAKE OVER

The first 709's were scarcely installed when IBM, late in 1958, announced two all-transistorized computer systems in its new 7000 Series of machines, the 7090 for scientific computation and the 7070 for commercial data processing. Five times faster than the 709, the 7090 would contain 44,000 transistors instead of vacuum tubes, have a magnetic core memory of 32,768 words with access time of slightly over two-millionths of a second, and feature several improvements in magnetic tape drive. Among the latter was a two-channel sensing device to permit the reading assembly to switch to a more sensitive reading level if it failed to obtain a clear signal from a bit on the tape. There was also a new self-checking mechanism that would catch almost all errors made during the recording. Also new was a skip-forward arrangement to permit the read-write head assembly to sense and skip over faulty sections of the tape whenever they occurred.

In the 7000 Series of computers, the principle of modularity was carried even further than in the 700 Series. The miniaturization made possible by the substitution of solid-state devices for vacuum tubes made possible basic computer modules not much bigger than playing cards but with far greater capability and speed than vacuum tube modules. Plugged into sub-sections which made up increasingly larger sub-sections, the interchangeable, replaceable transistor modules substantially reduced maintenance problems.* An entire installation could even be switched over from one machine in the same family, a 7070 to a 7074, for example, in the customer's plant within 60 to 70 hours. To ensure that the reliability of the machines kept pace with their increased capability, IBM began to produce its own germanium transistors with better performance characteristics than the commercial variety used in small radios and other everyday products on the market.

The 7090 embodied so many new engineering approaches and components that a period of eighteen months elapsed between the announcement of the machine and its first installation. In the meantime, Control Data Corporation, Sperry Rand, Philco, Radio Corporation of America, and other companies entered the market with transistorized computers. Despite the competition, the 7090 enjoyed such wide acceptance, when it appeared in mid-1960, that it soon became the most widely used large-scale scientific computing system in the world and the standard by which other computing systems were measured.**

WHAT PRICE ARITHMETIC

Early in 1963, IBM announced the 7094-II, a computer which was to be both the final and the most powerful machine in the famed 7000 Series. In order to place its performance in

* In addition, transistors develop little or no heat in operation, thus reducing the need for air-conditioning the computers. Heat had been responsible for many failures in earlier machines.

** 7090's were used at Cape Canaveral and Goddard Space Flight Center to process data on Project Mercury space probes; to help design the Saturn V space rocket for the National Aeronautics and Space Administration; and to process data for the North American Air Defense Command's Ballistics Missile Early Warning System (BMEWS).

proper perspective, it is necessary to glance back at the pioneering machines of a decade earlier. Where the 701 astonished users by performing 17,000 additions (or 2,200 multiplications) per second, the 7094-II made 357,000 additions (or 178,000 multiplications) per second. At their peak, machines of the 700 Series accomplished their calculations at an average cost of $1.25 per 100,000 (based on multiplications), as against $.25 per 100,000 for the 7094-II.

With the 7094-II, refinements possible within the existing framework of computer technology appeared to have reached a climax. The machine's access to core memory in less than two-millionths of a second and its internal circuitry enabling it to carry on simultaneous, *overlapping* operations at incredible speeds meant that it could be used effectively only by groups of customers willing to share its enormous resources. Units were installed at both the University of California's Western Data Processing Center and the Massachusetts Institute of Technology's Computation Center, where faculty and students from these institutions and others nearby made use of them for educational research projects.

NEXT, MICROELECTRONICS

In April, 1964, IBM surprised the computer industry with its "most important product announcement in company history." The product was a new line of computers, the IBM System 360, to be based on microelectronics. In the twenty years that had elapsed since Howard Aiken and I.B.M. had completed the Automatic Sequence Controlled Calculator and installed it at Harvard University, the company had been involved at virtually every level of computer engineering, from telephone relays and rotating switches, to vacuum tubes and wired circuits, to transistors and printed circuits. Now the company would move into the new world of "solid logic" technology with its chip transistors, resistors, diodes, and other diminutive components, all diffused through tiny pieces of germanium or silicon no more than a few hundredths of an inch square.

The drastic reduction in the physical size of the essential computer elements—the basic modules would now be about the size of dominoes—made possible by microelectronics increased still further the calculating speed. Millions of computations could now be accomplished in a second at a cost of about 3 cents per 100,000 for multiplications. Internal computer speeds of 1½ *nanoseconds* (billionths of a second) had been achieved. To match the pace, new devices for memory storage which could outstrip the access times provided by magnetic cores were being developed. Predictions were made of further breakthroughs in computer technology which would dwarf anything achieved so far in both speed and capability.

From its position as leader of the computer industry, IBM could look ahead toward the new developments with confidence and look back with satisfaction at the incredible dynasty of hardware and programming it had founded. From the day when the first 701 was completed in the spring of 1953 to the day when the last 7094-II left the company's production line late in 1966, an estimated thirty thousand of the IBM 700-7000 Series computers were either installed or on order for government agencies, scientific laboratories, business offices, hospitals, colleges, data processing centers, and other users throughout the United States. According to some informed estimates, the company accounted for about 70 per cent of the nation's total computer business.

As the second Industrial Revolution swept relentlessly ahead, the editors of the *Harvard Business Review* could observe with awe the extent to which their astute prediction of 1954 had come true, and with surprise the extraordinary degree to which its realization was the handiwork of a single United States company.

the
newest wonders
of the world

IT HAS BEEN OBSERVED, somewhat wryly, that an electrical engineer of the early twentieth century would be far more mystified by the modern transistor than Imhotep himself would be by the Empire State Building. This comparison may be a kind of inside joke among structural engineers who know Imhotep as the first engineer in recorded history, but it has a certain amount of historical truth. For unlike other branches of the engineering art, structural engineering—the most ancient of them all—evolved with glacial slowness from basic principles discovered thousands of years ago up until the middle of the last century. Almost five thousand years have passed since Imhotep directed the building of the step pyramid at Sakkara, but the Egyptians, using only their primitive pulleys, windlasses, capstans, and plentiful manpower, would have been perfectly capable of putting up a 50-story skyscraper. Bridges constructed in 1800 B.C. were not basically different from those erected in A.D. 1800. The ancient Greeks were masters of the column and knew how to make and work steel. The Romans, who built the arch and the dome to perfection, discovered concrete well before the time of Christ. Even the cathedrals of the Middle Ages were built—with a few improvements—on essentially the same principles as those employed by the Greeks and the Romans.

In the last half of the nineteenth century, however, there took place a burst of creativity in structural engineering that amounted to a mutation. Stemming from the discovery in England in 1824 of portland cement and in 1856 of the Bessemer process for making cheap steel, there came, all within a few decades, the steel cable, the wide-flanged steel girder, the cantilevered span, and the reinforced concrete slab. Structures became possible, such as the Eiffel Tower and the great steel domed exhibition building at Lyons, the variety of which seemed limited only by the imagination. In the United States alone, between 1867 and 1883, there were in construction *simultaneously* the first all-steel bridge, the first multiple-story building with a steel frame, the first large cable-suspension bridge, and the first cantilevered bridge.* By the turn of the century, construction had begun in Cincinnati on the first reinforced concrete office building, the Ingalls Building.

The fruits of this late-dawning Golden Age of structural engineering transformed whole areas of the United States within one generation, and there seems to be no end yet even to the beginning. Continuing advances in structural materials, techniques, and design are stimulating taller and larger buildings, longer bridges, bolder architectural forms than would have been attempted as recently as a decade ago. Outstanding among these developments are the use of prestressed concrete, high-strength steels and steel bolts, and wind- and earthquake-resistant

* These were in order: the Eads Bridge over the Mississippi at St. Louis; the Home Insurance Company Building in Chicago; the Brooklyn Bridge; the Kentucky River Viaduct.

construction. Together, they are helping to create the face of tomorrow.

STRENGTH THROUGH STRESS

Most visitors to New York's International Airport are startled to see what appears to be either an enormous stone bird or a great plane of fantastic design hovering among the buildings surrounding the central arrival area. But it is not a bird, or a plane. It is Trans-World Airline's recently completed passenger terminal, and a prime example of the strategic use of materials and construction techniques without which such a design would have been virtually impossible. One of the materials, prestressed concrete, is at once so strong and so flexible that it can be used for everything from ponderous bridge piles to the airy geometry of fair pavilions. This versatility is based on a deceptively simple principle: that stress introduced into concrete will counteract stress produced later by the loads it must carry.

The principle itself is far from new and was probably first uncovered by a gunsmith of the early fifteenth century when he found that a gun barrel could be strengthened by placing heated steel bands around it and allowing them to cool and contract. When a powder charge was later exploded in the barrel, the compressive strength added by the bands served to counteract the expansive pressure from within. Much the same idea occurred four centuries later to experimenters seeking to reinforce the low tensile strength of concrete by the use of embedded steel rods. They reasoned that if the rods were stretched under tension, then released when the concrete had hardened around them, the contraction of the rods would compress the concrete more densely. This "built-in" compressive stress was expected to offset later tensile stress produced by loads on the concrete part. Although the theory was sound, the steel rods used at the time would "yield," or stretch a bit, at a stress of about 30,000 pounds per square inch. At this rate, the "creep" of concrete under load would release the prestress, wiping out any advantage to be gained.

By the end of World War II, however, high-strength steel wires and bars with working stresses of well over 100,000 pounds per square inch, providing great elasticity, had been applied for use in prestressing, and interest in the technique revived sharply. For the high-strength steel tendons could be worked to five or six times the stress previously allowable, thus conserving steel. At the same time, less concrete would usually be needed to make a structural unit, such as a beam, since the entire cross section of the prestressed beam would resist loads, instead of only the relatively small compression area at the top as in a conventional beam. A still further advantage of prestressing was that the tensed steel wires running through the concrete would keep it from cracking later under working loads—a long-standing complaint against concrete structures.

All of these new attractions of prestressing, when added to concrete's well known durability, fire and corrosion resistance, and low cost, stimulated a flurry of developmental activity in the 1940's, out of which came a major breakthrough: the perfection of a prestressed concrete bridge pile, by the Raymond Concrete Pile Company of New York, that opened up a useful new approach to long-bridge, multiple-span construction. Traditionally, concrete piles had been used as foundations sunk below the mudline of a riverbed to support piers carrying the actual load of the bridge. But the new prestressed concrete piles, because of their great resistance to bending and cracking, could serve both as foundations carrying the *vertical* load of the bridge and as free-standing structural members capable of absorbing all the formidable *horizontal* forces of water currents, waves, wind, and actual collision. Since the piles could also be economically precast on a production-line basis to any length, diameter, number, strength of concrete, or degree of prestressing required, they could be used for high or low bridges, trestle spans, causeways, breakwaters, piers, highway overpasses, on land or in marshes, bogs, shallow or deep water.

THE LONGEST BRIDGE IN THE WORLD

The development of the prestressed concrete pile set construction engineers free to proceed with undertakings that had for years been considered hopelessly impractical—technically, or economically, or both. Among these was a scheme to build a bridge across Lake Pontchartrain connecting New Orleans with the heavily populated north shore of the 600 square-mile lake. Early in 1955, a group of contractors and engineers, using a design based on precast, prestressed concrete piles and road slabs, began construction of the 24-mile bridge and completed it in a little over a year for the frugal sum of $27 million.*

Behind this impressive performance was a master plan: the bridge was to be built in 2,215 identical sections, known as "bents," at the rate of eight bents a day. Since each individual bent consisted of two 30-ton prestressed concrete piles, a 30-ton concrete cap connecting them, and a 185-ton prestressed concrete slab to go across the top forming the roadbed, the construction schedule thus called for the *production and installation* of 32 huge concrete components each day.

To meet this extremely demanding program, a mass production technique was worked out. Piles were cast in sections, then joined together later in whatever lengths were required for the particular set of bents to be built. Before concrete was cast for each section, longitudinal rods were placed in the casting frame to leave apertures through which the prestressing wires would be threaded later. After the concrete had set, and the rods were removed, the finished sections were aligned end to end and their

* The contractors were Brown & Root, Inc., Houston, Texas, and T. L. James and Company, Ruston, Louisiana; the structural engineers, Palmer & Baker, Inc., Mobile, Alabama.

longitudinal holes matched up. The end section surfaces were sealed together by a strong polyester resin glue, stressing cables were passed through the lengthwise holes of the entire pile assembly and then tensioned by hydraulic jacks to approximately 25 tons each. The ends were next anchored by plates to the concrete, and cement was forced into the holes to fill the spaces around the cables. After a final setting period, the anchors were removed, *transferring* the prestressing from the wires to the concrete through the bonding action of the cement.

In much the same way, the road slabs were made in casting forms with 175 prestressing wires strung through the form and concrete poured around the whole. When the huge monolith had hardened sufficiently to be removed from the form, the prestressing wires were pulled simultaneously by jacks and anchored in place until concrete strength of 3,000 pounds per square inch had been reached. The strands were then cut and the slab was ready for use just as it was. The pile caps—the third basic element—were made of ordinary reinforced concrete, each cap with special extending rods that would penetrate down several feet into the tops of the two piles it was to connect.

By the spring of 1955, as piles, slabs, and caps began to stack up like enormous building blocks at the casting yard on the north shore of Lake Pontchartrain, the time came to start building the bridge. For the engineers who had planned ahead so precisely, it was in every sense the moment of truth. For despite the care taken to make sure that all the parts would be precast to the closest possible tolerances, there was no certainty that during installation the huge piles could all be driven to within a few *inches* of specifications, or that the caps would all be less than one-eighth of an inch out of place—the maximum permissible—or that the bearing plates on the bottoms of the slabs would all sit so squarely that anchor bolts on the caps below could be threaded exactly through them. But after the first piles had been driven in the north end of the lake, and as work proceeded smoothly, without complication, day after day, in an arrow-straight line toward the south shore, the engineers began to perceive the extent of their achievement.

In all, only one set of pile driving equipment, one set of cap placing machines, and one slab-setting rig were required in the whole construction period. Since no problem ever arose making it necessary for the equipment to back up, the operation became continuous, with the pile driving sometimes as much as two miles ahead of the cap setting and three miles ahead of the slab setting. So nearly complete was each section of the bridge as it was placed that workmen could drive in the morning from the north shore of the lake onto the last slab set the previous day. When the final slab was put in place in early August, 1956, little more than fourteen months had elapsed since the first piles were driven for the longest bridge that had ever been built.

The Lake Pontchartrain Bridge was the forerunner of a whole group of prestressed concrete spans, including the noble Lake Maracaibo Bridge, with its concrete piers soaring 148 feet above the water, and the 12-mile trestle of the monumental Chesapeake Bay Bridge–Tunnel—the longest such combination in the world. Using the experience gained from these and other projects involving huge masses of prestressed concrete, engineers began to experiment with the material in more limited quantities, calling on its strength to create key supporting members for structures of far more intricate and advanced design.*

TENSION IN THE SERVICE OF ART

Architects *think* in materials, the poet Paul Valéry pointed out a half-century ago. He was referring at the time to Monsieur Eiffel and his famous fantasy in iron and steel, but the observation

---

* One of these, the concrete runway extension at LaGuardia Airport in New York, required 13,000 prestressed concrete slabs capable of supporting 200,000 pounds, to stand up under the strain of jet traffic. It was the largest precast, prestressed, post-tensioned project of this kind ever undertaken in the United States.

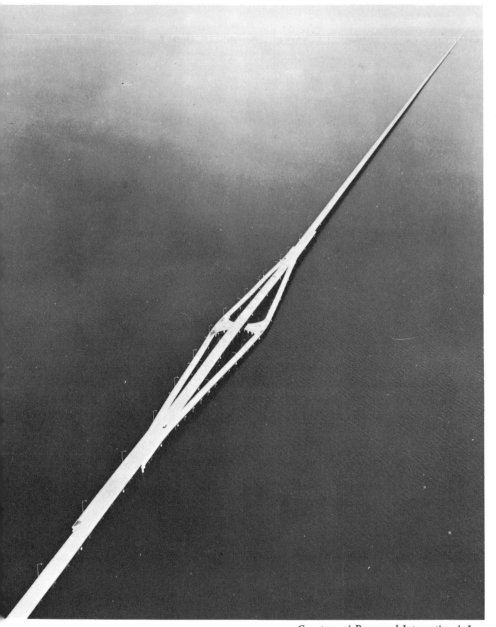

Lake Pontchartrain Bridge

is even truer today. Eero Saarinen, designer of Trans-World's spectacular "bird in flight" terminal, could have been thinking only in concrete when he envisioned the four soaring parabolic spans that cantilever winglike more than 80 feet beyond their central supporting buttresses to form the roof of the building. Since the spans are made of 5,000 tons of concrete reinforced with 750 tons of steel—and there are no columns anywhere in the building—the four Y-shaped buttresses *alone* carry not only the total weight of the roof, but also the horizontal load caused by the outward thrust of the cantilevered spans.

Most visitors accept this fact without wonderment. What few would have any reason to know, as they stand admiring the arching 50-foot vaults over their heads, is that the stability of the entire structure depends on *four* post-tensioned concrete ties under their feet. For among the myriad engineering perplexities posed by the Saarinen design was the basic problem of how to stabilize the geometry of the building by linking the four separate buttresses so securely that they could absorb both the vertical load, as well as the enormous horizontal load pulling them apart, within tolerable limits. Clearly, any such linking members would have to be capable of withstanding the great tension involved without stretching to any appreciable degree. Even the strongest steel made could not be used alone for the purpose because of its relatively high elasticity. But if strong steel bars were encased in concrete, then *post-tensioned,* the mass area of the concrete acting at low compressive stresses would serve to counteract the elastic extension of the steel.

Proceeding along these lines, the structural engineers for the building, Ammann and Whitney, linked the four buttresses at their foundations with multiple sets of 1¼-inch stress steel bars, then covered them with cast-in-place concrete. When the material had hardened sufficiently, hydraulic jacks were used to apply tension to the bars, which were then anchored to the ends of the concrete ties by bearing plates, and the jacks released. The tension, transferred to the concrete through the anchorage plates, served to balance the force of the roof to the point where the largest tie could withstand a horizontal load of well over *2,000 tons*.

The ties of the TWA terminal stand as a shining example of the strategic use of post-tensioned concrete for buildings of daring design. Another is the strikingly original Assembly Hall of the University of Illinois at Urbana, which boasts the world's largest edge-supported dome.* Made of concrete, it rests like a huge inverted saucer atop another saucer containing the performance area and seating for 18,000 people. Where the edges of the saucers meet 42 feet above the ground, a ring girder of post-tensioned concrete contains the horizontal thrust of the 4,400-ton dome and transmits the vertical load through to 48 buttresses spaced around the base of the lower saucer. To create the ring girder, a concrete rim was poured at the grandstand level, then wrapped around with 2,467 turns (500 miles) of quarter-inch steel wire stressed to 120,000 pounds per square inch by special machinery circling the perimeter. By keeping the dome section and the bowl section in equilibrium, the ring girder made it possible to eliminate both interior and exterior columns entirely, thereby providing unobstructed vision from every seat in the hall. Beautiful, functional, and the pride of the Urbana campus, the Assembly Hall is an exciting illustration of what can be done with concrete—and imagination.

R EJUVENATION IN NUTS AND BOLTS

The idea that there could be anything new or unusual about nuts and bolts seems as unlikely as that something exhilarating could happen to the safety pin. Yet it is a fact that one of the most important current trends in structural engineering is the use of inch-thick high-strength steel bolts to join together pre-

---

* The architect was Max Abramovitz; and the structural engineers, Ammann and Whitney of New York.

Courtesy of the University of Illinois at Urbana

Assembly Hall, University of Illinois at Urbana

fabricated building components right at job site and to do it more quickly, reliably, cheaply, and quietly than in any other way. To construction engineers, these are qualities as admirable as those of the wheel must have seemed to the ancient Babylonians. As a matter of fact, the field bolting technique has made possible the erection of very large buildings that would otherwise be extremely difficult or absolutely out of the question.

The new status for nuts and bolts began in the 1950's when an acute shortage of trained riveters, as well as some serious deficiencies in rivets themselves, prompted the search for a substitute. Long experience with rivets had shown that in addition to the ear-splitting noise involved in installing them, their initial tensile strength after cooling was often not great enough to resist the loads upon them. The result was that after a while they tended to loosen, vibrate, and eventually require replacement. Engineers at work on substitutes reasoned that if frictional resistance could be built up sufficiently within the two parts of a connection, it would serve to prevent later slippage in spite of load. Since the nut-bolt arrangement is a very common friction type fastener, developing its resistance through its threads, it offered an obvious key to the problem. However, two further developments were required: the bolts would have to be strong enough to support the loads transferred from one large structural member to another—as between a girder and a column—and a means would have to be found to tighten the bolts in such a way as to create maximum frictional resistance. Research produced the answers: bolts made of very high-strength heat-treated alloy steel base material could be produced to withstand as much as 125,000 to 150,000 pounds of pressure per square inch; by special power-driven impact or torque wrenches, they could be tightened to any degree of tension required. More progress followed in the 1960's with the introduction of bolts with large hexagonal heads that completely eliminated the need for washers, and with the use of even higher strength steel.

THE LARGEST BUILDING IN THE WORLD

Among those who saw the heaven-sent advantages of high-strength steel bolts for their purposes were the engineers charged with the task of constructing the Vehicle Assembly Building at the John F. Kennedy Space Center on Merritt Island, Florida.* The building, which was to be used by the National Aeronau-

* This group of engineers was known as URSAM, composed of representatives of the Office of Max O. Urbahn; Roberts & Schaefer Company; Seelye Stevenson Value & Knecht; and Meuser, Rutledge, Wentworth & Johnson, all of New York.

tics and Space Administration to assemble the three stages of the Saturn V rocket and the Apollo spacecraft into a vehicle to take men to the moon, was to have some almost incredible features: it was to be as tall (526 feet) as the Washington Monument in order to permit the vertical assembly of the rocket; contain the greatest volume of enclosed space on record (125 million cubic feet) to provide room and equipment for 2,400-man crews; and have the biggest doors ever built (large enough to admit a 45-story building) in order to pass the space vehicle, atop its broad movable platform, when the time came to go to the launching pad several miles away. In addition, the building had to be constructed to withstand wind forces up to hurricane level without swaying more than 6 inches in any direction, since motion past that point might damage the space vehicle.* As if all this weren't enough, the building also had to be efficiently laid out, lend itself to future expansion and be completed within thirteen months.

Faced with these remarkable requirements, the engineers concluded, early on, that their goal for the Vehicle Assembly Building could not be the usual one of a simple building, at minimum cost, satisfying the esthetic tastes of architects and public alike. Instead, the structure would have to be planned empirically, for the complex purpose at hand, around multiple, uniform parts prefabricated as completely as possible in the shop, then joined together as quickly as possible in the field. And the key to this scheme was to make use on a grand scale of the technique of high-strength steel bolting. Following this plan, the engineers created a gigantic, boxlike building whose internal structure consists of two huge E-shaped steel frames, built back-to-back and connected there at intervals by floors to allow passage of men and equipment between them. By means of this arrange-

---

* Wind forces also dictated that only one of the great doors (which take nearly an hour to raise) should be opened on gusty days, and none when the wind velocity passed 63 miles per hour.

ment, the areas within the projecting prongs of the E's form compact, closely-associated working bays for the rocket assembly operations. The steel frames themselves are made up, honeycomb fashion, of individual structural modules formed of giant column sections* spaced 38 feet apart and bolted together with vertical, horizontal, and diagonal trusses in multiples of 38 feet. Together, these modules produce a three-dimensional steel frame that provides the great strength needed to carry the vertical and horizontal loads of the building, the optimum stiffness against wind pressures, and the adaptability for future extensions and additions. Enclosing the great box are more than a million square feet of aluminum panels, bolted to the outside of the steel skeleton. All in all, a total of *over one million* high-strength steel bolts were used to join together the 45,000 steel parts and other components that make up the Vehicle Assembly Building. Like a huge Meccano-set marvel, it towers today beside the broad Banana River northwest of the launching site at Cape Kennedy, where, even in that area of fantastic structures, it dwarfs everything in sight.

While the V.A.B., as it is known, is a virtual showcase for high-strength steel bolts in large buildings, other impressive examples abound. The Verrazano-Narrows Bridge, the longest suspension bridge in the world, contains nearly 3,800 *tons* of high-strength steel bolts in its suspended structure, approaches, anchorages, and cables. The new Chase Manhattan Bank Building, an impressive 813-foot structure, was erected on less than an acre of ground directly in the heart of New York's congested Wall Street area in record time through a combination of precise logistics, prefabricated structural components, and field bolting. Great column sections weighing up to 52 tons were manufactured in Philadelphia, shipped to New York, swung high into the sky like so many matchsticks above the heads of passersby below,

---

* These column sections, weighing 734 pounds per lineal foot, were the largest ever rolled by the steel industry.

then fastened into place with a total of 640,000 steel bolts by crews perching in mid-air.

Similarly, Chicago's new 1,100-foot John Hancock Center—the tallest building ever raised up in that wind-buffeted city—makes use of an unusual design calling for exterior steel columns connected by diagonal sections which act as inclined columns, carrying their share of the gravity load.* The joints at the intersections of the columns and diagonals are prefabricated in the shop, but field connections of the primary structural members are made by some 130,000 high-strength steel bolts. The extreme rigidity of this system makes it possible to use only as much steel per square foot of floor area as would be required for a 35-story, conventional framed building. With 34 floors at the bottom devoted to offices, and 49 floors at the top set aside for lofty apartments, the Hancock Center offers an ingenious solution to the noise, fumes, glare, and other inconveniences of modern city living. Its 1,800-feet-per-minute elevators (the fastest in the world), swimming pool in the sky, and self-contained parking system offer a fascinating glimpse into the future for metropolis dwellers everywhere.

REACHING FOR THE SKY

Putting up tall buildings seems to be such an obsession with Americans that students of architecture have evolved a theory about it. The tower, they say, has consistently stood as a symbol of power down through the ages—from the tall tips of Chinese pagodas, the spires of Gothic cathedrals, the high campaniles of medieval Italy, to the modern skyscraper. If this is true, then it is not surprising that from the instant inexpensive steel came onto the market in the United States near the turn of the century, American builders not only recognized its potentialities for tall buildings, but virtually hustled them into reality. The first of

* This office-apartment building was constructed for the John Hancock Insurance Company by Skidmore, Owings and Merrill, Chicago.

all skyscrapers, the 10-story Home Insurance Company building in Chicago, wound up with a metal frame composed of five
bottom floors of wrought iron beams and five top floors of steel
beams because the latter become available when the building
was half finished. By the early 1900's, a dizzy height of 20 stories
had been reached in New York's Flatiron Building, and by 1913
the Woolworth Building towered a daring 60 stories over lower
Manhattan. During the 1920's the city was caught up in a skyscraper boom that finally tapered off in 1929 with the 77-story
Chrysler Building, and culminated in the stunning achievement
of the 102-story Empire State Building in 1931.

Yet despite the difference in height, all of these buildings
were basically alike in structural organization. At each floor
level, vertical steel column sections were riveted to horizontal
steel floor beams to form cubes of space from one side of the
building to the other. This rigid steel "eggcrate" frame carried
both the weight of the building and the lateral load imposed by
the wind. The outside wall of brick or stone was simply attached
like a curtain to the steel frame to provide stiffening and to enclose and insulate the interior. The great amount of steel used
in these frames was held to be mandatory if tall buildings were to
support the accumulated weight of their multiple floors and resist
the terrific force of winds battering their slender, vulnerable
profiles. Besides their structural similarity, the skyscrapers were
also alike in their heavy dependency on continuing advance-
ments in the development of high-speed elevator systems.

"Curtain wall" construction, as it was called, dominated tall
building design in the United States for nearly three-quarters of
a century, even though it had some major disadvantages. For
one thing, the forest of interior columns created by the eggcrate
frame cut heavily into available floorspace. For another, the
growing variety of utilities required—elevators, electricity, heat-
ing, ventilating, and air conditioning—stole progressively more
room from the rentable total. Often as little as *half* of the interior

space of a skyscraper turned out to be usable for offices. Clearly, a new approach was needed—and it finally was found. By the early 1960's, increasing knowledge of structural dynamics and of the design capabilities of new building materials began to yield some radically new theories about tall building construction. Outstanding among these was the concept of using high-strength steels to make large structural building components.* Architects and engineers working with the carbon, heat-treated-carbon, alloy and heat-treated-alloy steels coming onto the market reasoned that advantage could be taken of the greater strength of the new materials to reduce considerably the size and weight of column sections, beams, trusses, panels, etc., thereby cutting overall building costs. Moreover, the strength of these parts was such that their use in the *exterior wall of a building alone* would provide sufficient strength to carry both the vertical load of gravity and the lateral load of wind, making it possible to eliminate interior columns completely.

The first building to put these radical new precepts into practice was the pioneering International Business Machines Building in Pittsburgh, which had an exterior "bearing" wall built entirely of diagonal trusses prefabricated of high-strength steels with yields up to 100,000 pounds per square inch and no interior columns at all.** Completed in 1962, the building gave the skyscraper a new lease on life in two ways. Its exterior "bearing wall" construction broke ground for the design of many advanced new buildings, including the John Hancock Center in Chicago. At the same time, its use of high-strength steel com-

---

* Standard structural steels withstand loads up to 36,000 pounds per square inch before they begin to "yield," or stretch slightly. High-strength structural steels are generally considered those with yields of between 42,000 and 100,000 pounds per square inch.

** The architect was Curtis & Davis, New Orleans and New York; the structural engineers, Worthington, Skilling, Helle and Jackson, New York. So proud was the steel fabricator of his part in this building that he painted each grade of steel a different color to call public attention to the innovation.

ponents in the exterior wall provided the key to the construction of New York's new quarter-mile-high, half-billion-dollar World Trade Center, a power symbol of a magnitude not likely to be challenged in the foreseeable future.*

THE TALLEST TOWERS IN THE WORLD

As might be expected—much to the chagrin of the owners of the Empire State Building—the main feature of the World Trade Center is not one, but *two* 110-story towers, thrusting 1,350 feet into the sky over lower Manhattan. The great square towers, containing offices devoted to international trade, are surrounded by four low-rise buildings, including a new United States Customs Building and a hotel, all facing on a central plaza. With a total floor space of 12 million square feet—the equivalent of a half-dozen Rockefeller Centers—and a working population of 50,000 people, the Center anticipates even more than that number of daily visitors curious to see the tallest buildings in the world. Many will aim directly for the observation decks of the towers so that they can see 45 miles in every direction. But some may first pause, bemused at the sight of what appear to be two giant, shiny steel and glass boxes poised airily on top of a few dozen thin, tapering columns. At closer inspection, each of these columns will be seen to branch into three others that rise all the way to the top, creating frames as they go for thousands of long, curiously narrow windows—like the fenestration of a great battlement. The surprisingly elegant effect, a synthesis of solid mass and graceful line, is at the same time a remarkable exercise in structural ingenuity. Both depend, to an extent never before attempted in a building, on the use of high-strength steel.

The walls of the towers are, in essence, great steel lattices put

---

* The architect was Minoru Yamasaki, of Detroit; and the structural engineers were Worthington, Skilling, Helle and Jackson, of Seattle, for the Port of New York Authority. Now under construction, the Center is expected to be completed in 1972.

together in three-story-high prefabricated sections.* Each section is composed of three, foot-square steel box columns tied together by horizontal steel panels at the floor levels. At the lowest floors, where the gravity loads accumulate, the sections are made of steel with yields of strengths up to 100,000 pounds per square inch. As the wall rises, the gravity load decreases but the wind load builds up, and a whole spectrum of steels is called into play. At the top third of the tower, sections made of standard steel provide sufficient strength to resist the main force of the wind. All told, a total of twelve different grades of steel go into the 4,800 sections that make up the walls of the towers, necessitating calculations so complex that computers were used to break the problem down into two stages. First, the machines processed data on wind velocity probabilities for the area from 120 different wind directions; on the dynamics and aerodynamics of height; and on acceptable levels of human response to the motion of buildings. When the results showed how much the building could be allowed to move without sacrificing safety or comfort, the machines then computed the precise width, length, thickness, and grade of steel to be used in each prefabricated section of both buildings. This information was supplied by the engineers directly to the fabricators on the computer punch cards, eliminating for the first time many of the intermediate steps of making and checking engineering and shop drawings.

The mosaic-like steel bearing wall built up in this painstaking way is so strong that it carries both the horizontal loads of hurricane winds and nearly half of the total weight of the building as well. The balance of the weight is supported by heavy steel columns enclosing a central core containing the utilities, elevator shafts, stairwells, etc. In between, connecting the outside bearing wall with the utility core columns, are prefabricated 60-foot floor sections containing electrical, air-conditioning, and

---

* The use of prefabricated parts reduced the number of components that have to be installed to about 10 per cent of the total.

other components already installed in their webs. The beauty of this structural arrangement lies in its effectiveness in saving precious floor space: the high-strength steel bearing wall eliminates all interior columns except the few around the utility core; the core concentrates all its equipment in one central area; the pre-packaged floor beams eliminate space beneath them usually set aside for utility connections. An essential feature is the high-speed elevator system rushing express passengers to lobbies at midway points up in the towers for transfer to locals serving the floors in between, as in the subway system.

The result? Nearly 80 per cent of the floor space of the towers will be income-producing—a statistic as admirable in its way as the building's deceptively fragile, espaliered columns are in theirs. By overcoming the structural and economic obstacles that have blocked progress in tall buildings for the last forty years, the World Trade Center puts the skyscraper back in business.

DEFYING NATURE BY DESIGN

Building a skyscraper in New York, while expensive, is not otherwise considered a risky business. Putting one up in Mexico City is something else again, as anyone knows who visited there in the late summer of 1957. For on July 28 of that year, in the dark hours of the early morning, two great earth tremors shook southern and central Mexico, felling adobe huts, cathedrals, factories, hotels, office buildings, and apartments in an area that reached from Mexico City to Acapulco, 300 miles away. In all, 125 dead and many millions of dollars of property damage were the toll of the worst earthquake to hit Mexico since records were first kept in 1900. In Mexico City, amid the shattered glass, buckled sidewalks, ruptured water lines, crumbled masonry, and twisted steel girders that disfigured the central business section, only the newly-built, 43-story Latino Americana Tower, the tallest building in Latin America, escaped with not even a broken windowpane to show for the violence it had undergone. Recording instruments in the tower, examined after the quake, revealed that at the peak of the vibrations, the top had whiplashed back and forth about a foot every two seconds, resisting lateral forces of over 40 tons that threatened to snap it off altogether.

The survival of the Latino Americana Tower was accounted for by its earthquake-resistant construction based on an aseismic design, developed at the University of Illinois, that was being tried out for the first time in a major building.* A harsher testing ground could scarcely have been found, for Mexico City is located on extremely soft clay filling in the dry bed of old Lake Texcoco. Throughout the clay basin, the water level is within a few feet of the surface, and as the table falls because of the pumping of water, buildings on ordinary foundations sink as much as 8 inches a year. Buildings on piles fare not much better, sometimes ending up with first floors left high and dry several feet above the ground. At the site of the Latino Americana Tower itself, the engineers found that watery clay extended to a depth of 100 feet or so below the surface, and that below this were layers of sand, gravel, and more clay scarcely promising for a building that was to be twice as tall as any in the city and earthquake-resistant into the bargain. In the absence of the good bedrock they wanted, the engineers were obliged to devise a compromise. To counter the settlement problem, they planned to drive 361 sturdy concrete piles to a depth of 117 feet in order to carry the load of the building down to the relatively more stable sand and gravel level. On top of the piles they would place a foundation for the building made up of a grid of large concrete girders reinforced with steel bars 1½ inches in

---

* Dr. Nathan Newmark, head of the University's Civil Engineering Department at Urbana, served as consultant on the design of the building, and two of his former students worked with him on the project. Chief designer was Eduardo Espinosa, and chief engineer for the owner of the building was Adolfo Zeevaert, both of Mexico City.

diameter. This big box would then *float* on the subsurface "soup." On the foundation, they would erect the tower's 3,600-ton steel framework, stiffened at all its connections to reduce lateral quake movements.

The tower itself was to rise in four tiers: the first 120 feet square, the second 90 feet square, the main tower 70 feet square, and the topmost section tapering almost to a point. Throughout, the floors were to be made of 3½-inch-thick concrete slabs reinforced lengthwise, crosswise, and on the diagonal with steel bars. To help resist horizontal torsion during quakes, the slabs were to be firmly attached to the steel frame both by special heavy steel anchorages and by welding the diagonal reinforcing bars to steel hoops around the column sections of the frame. Partitions on each floor would be connected to the floors, but their tops would be joined to the upper slabs with flexible hangars. Windows were to have clearances of from ½ to 2½ inches in their frames and extra large pivots to prevent them from coming out when the frames were distorted. By means of all of these connections, the components of the building would be tied together so securely that the whole would move together as a unit under stress, instead of pulling apart at the seams.

In arriving at this basic design for the tower, the most crucial problem for the engineers had been the business of planning ahead for the unknown dynamic forces to which the building might be subjected. Records had shown that earthquakes of intensities up to Number Seven on the Modified Mercalli Intensity Scale had actually occurred several times in Mexico City and that quakes of Intensity Eight *might* occur.* In this case, the building would have to be designed to withstand vibrations as frequently as every 1½ to 2½ seconds and ground motion of from 3 to 6 inches per second. But this amount of information was far from enough. The vibration characteristics of the tower

---

* The scale has a total of 12 degrees of intensity, ranging from scarcely-felt vibrations to total devastation.

itself would also have to be calculated, since the greatest stress of all would result if the pulses from the convulsive ground motion were reinforced within the building. Studies, which were then undertaken to learn how the building might be expected to vibrate, showed that it would, theoretically, have a resonance of about 2 cycles per second.

In addition, since it was a rule of thumb that the horizontal force produced by a quake would act on every part of a building in proportion to its weight, a value for the maximum expected force had to be assigned. Under the prevailing Mexico City building code, this value was placed arbitrarily at 2½ per cent, that is, structural members at any floor level were expected to be able to withstand horizontal forces equal to 2½ per cent of all the vertical •loads above that level. But since the Latino Americana Tower was to be so unusually high, the engineers decided to boost this seismic coefficient in order to be on the safe side. They proceeded to double it to 5 per cent for structural members in the lower part of the building, where the "shearing" forces would be the greatest, and increased it gradually over the height to 19 per cent in the upper floors near the tower. So constructed, the building would withstand damage to the point where even relatively minor repairs would be unnecessary if the expected earthquake occurred.

With the aseismic design finally determined, construction on the Latino Americana Tower began in 1949 and was completed early in 1957. In the summer of 1956, in a paper presented to the World Conference on Earthquake Engineering at Berkeley, California, two of the consulting engineers on the project observed: "It appears that the structure is adequately safe for the maximum probable earthquake in Mexico City and has a safety factor of about two for the maximum earthquake which has occurred in the period from 1900 to 1956, based on working stresses. The actual factor of safety is, of course, considerably greater." One year later, they were proved right. The 1957 quake reached an intensity of between Seven and Eight on the Mercalli Scale, with ground waves peaking at between 1 and 1.8 seconds.

When the fearful ordeal was ended, and the engineers rushed to examine the recording instruments mounted at various elevations in the building, they learned that while the sway at the very top of the tower had reached *12 inches,* displacement at the other levels had not exceeded the design values. The tower had completely vindicated its design, successfully undergoing almost exactly the forces it had been engineered to withstand. In so doing, it offered invaluable design criteria and construction guidelines for use in all the seismic countries of the world, thus demonstrating once again that engineering is the science of controlling nature—even at her most intractable—for the good of men everywhere.

acknowledgements

INVALUABLE ASSISTANCE in the preparation of this book was provided by the following individuals, who offered guidance, perceptive comments, and many helpful suggestions.

Boyd Anderson *Ammann & Whitney, New York, N.Y.*
Dr. Werner Buchholz *Evaluation Development Manager, IBM Systems Development Division, Poughkeepsie, N.Y.*
Chester F. Carlson *Pittsford, N.Y.*
Dr. Harold Clark *Manager of Scientific Liaison Office, Xerox Corporation, Rochester, N.Y.*
William H. Cook *Head of Product Development, SST, The Boeing Company, Renton, Wash.*
W. F. Cronin *Manager, Seattle District, General Electric Company, Seattle, Wash.*
Dr. Edward E. David, Jr. *Executive Director, Research, Communications Research Division, Bell Telephone Laboratories, Murray Hill, N.J.*

163

Dr. John H. Dessauer *Executive Vice President of Research & Advanced Engineering, Xerox Corporation, Rochester, N.Y.*

Professor James M. Dunford *Captain USNR, The Towne School of Civil & Mechanical Engineering, University of Pennsylvania, Philadelphia, Pa.*

R. D. Ehrbar *Department Head, Exchange Transmission Department, Bell Telephone Laboratories, Murray Hill, N.J.*

C. H. Elmendorf *Vice President—Engineering, American Telephone & Telegraph Company, New York, N.Y.*

Donald W. Finlay *Design Engineer, 747, The Boeing Company, Renton, Wash.*

Maurice Fornerod *Raymond International, Inc., New York, N.Y.*

Dr. Herman H. Goldstine *Director of Scientific Development, IBM Data Processing Division, White Plains, N.Y.*

Dr. Newman A. Hall *Executive Director, Commission on Engineering Education, Washington, D.C.*

B. D. Holbrook *Head, Computer Systems Research Department, Bell Telephone Laboratories, Murray Hill, N.J.*

Fazlur Khan *Skidmore, Owings & Merrill, Chicago, Ill.*

William P. Kimball *Assistant Secretary—Education, American Society of Civil Engineering, New York, N.Y.*

Dr. J. A. Kyger *Vice President and Chief Scientist, Avco Missiles, Space & Electronics Group, Wilmington, Mass.*

George C. Martin *Vice President—Engineering, The Boeing Company, Seattle, Wash.*

Clyde R. Mayo *Vice President, Business Products Systems Division, Xerox Corporation, Rochester, N.Y.*

E. T. Mottram *Director, Submarine Cable Laboratory, Bell Telephone Laboratories, Murray Hill, N.J. (Retired.)*

Dr. Nathan N. Newmark *Head, Department of Civil Engineering, University of Illinois, Urbana, Ill.*

Dudley Nichols *Chief Project Engineer 707-720, The Boeing Company, Renton, Wash.*

Robert Panoff *Principal Officer & Director, MPR Associates, Washington, D.C.*

Ralph Partridge *Main Memory Development Manager, IBM Systems Development Division, Poughkeepsie, N.Y.*

Dr. John R. Pierce *Executive Director, Research Communications Sciences Division, Murray Hill, N.J.*

Manfred H. Riedel *Seelye Stevenson Value & Knecht, New York, N.Y.*

Leslie E. Robertson *Worthington, Skilling, Helle & Jackson, New York, N.Y.*

Theodore Rockwell *Principal Officer & Director, MPR Associates, Washington, D.C.*

Louis H. Roddis, Jr. *Captain USNR, President, Pennsylvania Electric Company, a General Public Utilities Corporation subsidiary, Johnstown, Pa.*

George S. Schairer *Vice President—Research & Development, The Boeing Company, Seattle, Wash.*

Dr. F. A. Schwertz *Associate Manager of Research Laboratories, Xerox Corporation, Rochester, N.Y.*

Louis Voerman *Plant General Manager, IBM Systems Manufacturing Division, Poughkeepsie, N.Y.*

Lewis E. Walkup *Battelle Memorial Institute, Columbus, Ohio.*

Marvin Warner *Seelye Stevenson Value & Knecht, New York, N.Y.*

William A. Weimcr *Manager of Systems Engineering, IBM Data Processing Division, White Plains, N.Y.*

Warren F. Wilson *Flight Test Engineer, The Boeing Company, Renton, Wash.*

index